Tips & Traps
When Buying a Franchise

Second Edition

MARY E. TOMZACK

SOURCE BOOK PUBLICATIONS, OAKLAND

Source Book Publications
1814 Franklin St., # 820, Oakland, CA 94612
(510) 839-5471

10 9 8 7 6 5 4 3 2
Second Printing 2002

ISBN 1-887137-12-2

Original Cover Illustration: Wallop Manyum
Sponsoring Editor: Nicole Thompson

To two great women
my mother, Mary K. Tomzack
and my mother-in-law, Esther L. Goldschneider

PREFACE

Perhaps you are a casualty of the big business merger and acquisition mania or feel unappreciated and unfulfilled in your corporate position and would like to start a business of your own. Or maybe you're a woman or a member of an ethnic or racial minority and you're looking for the so-called "level playing field." Perhaps you're a recent college graduate or have worked only a few years and have decided that you already have the skills to operate your own business. Then again, you may already be in business for yourself, but not achieving the results you want. For all of you, and for others who simply want a chance at running your own business, a franchise business may be the solution.

During the last five or six years, while doing research for this book and operating my business, FranchiseHelp, Inc., I have had the pleasure of talking to hundreds of franchisees across the United States. Also, I have had the opportunity to interact with colleagues and other professionals in the franchise industry on a regular basis. The franchisee and industry expert interviews revealed many interesting insights "from those in the trenches," which I will share with you throughout the book.

But there is one overriding principle, which all the research and interviews bear out, and that is—*making the right initial choice of a franchise is 95% of the success recipe!* Of course, hard work and a good business sense are also necessary, but for the readers of this book we will take that as a given. I am convinced that, if you read this book carefully, and take the time to do the necessary investigation and analysis, your chances of success as a franchisee are assured.

Mary E. Tomzack

Acknowledgements

Updating and revising the original *Tips & Traps* book turned out to be a far more intensive and time-consuming project than I envisioned. The reward, for me, is a book that I believe will give prospective franchisees all the tools and insights needed to make a good decision.

I received a great deal of help from my staff at FranchiseHelp who assisted with the new research and, of course, the typing. Following are the individuals I want to especially thank:

- ❧ Dolores Leston, my invaluable assistant, and also, Ashley Abraham, Teresa Acocella, Scott Tomback, Michael Lawless and Velco Chemical's Christine Preiss.

- ❧ The editor of this book, Nicole Thompson, who suggested changes with professionalism and accuracy.

- ❧ The expertise of Richard Clapsaddle, Dan Lasman and Carl Carlsson is greatly appreciated.

Franchisees and franchise industry experts are all very busy individuals. You will find their comments, observations and advice throughout this book. There would be no book without their input and I am very grateful that they took the time to offer their advice.

Lastly, I want to thank my husband, Michel Goldschneider, for his unstinting support and also my children, Vanessa and Evan Goldschneider, for their enthusiasm and encouragement.

TABLE OF CONTENTS

Contents

1
FRANCHISING FOR THE 21ST CENTURY

When I wrote the first edition of this book in 1994, we had a somewhat different economic climate than we do now at the beginning of 1999. In 1994, Americans were just coming out of a weak economy and "corporate downsizing" was a phrase much bandied about by the media and the average person. Certainly, corporate workers who had been downsized or chose to leave their positions because of difficult situations were a big part of this period's phenomenal franchise growth. Conditions that influence franchising growth are very different today.

The last few years have been marked by a booming stock market and a U.S. population enjoying low unemployment and no inflation. Many franchisors have found that investors are reluctant to invest in a franchised business when all they have to do is sit back and watch their stock investments rise daily. The strong economy has also created a situation where fewer corporations are likely to lay off middle managers—those who were rushing to a variety of franchise opportunities a few years ago.

While many of the Asiatic economies, Russia and some Latin American countries are struggling with poor, almost defunct, economies, it is far from clear whether the U.S. economy will enter a downturn. It does appear that the well above average gains in the equity markets will level off. Many believe that investors will once again be willing to take prudent risks and invest in a franchise business. In other words, many individuals may return to making money "the old-fashioned way," through careful choices and hard work in their own businesses.

The evolving trend, which began at the beginning of the 1990s—that of the new franchisee who is a multi-unit owner or a developer of a large region or territory—continues and is even more pronounced. Surely, there will always be a place for the small, limited mom-and-pop operation, but the numbers are dwindling. The franchisee of the 21st century is very likely to be the owner and manager of a sizable corporate entity; most franchise systems are definitely encouraging this trend.

The strategy of co-branding, marrying two or more branded concepts and offering the goods and services in one location, is thriving. Co-branding was basically unknown at the time of this book's first edition. Chapter 9 discusses this exciting trend. It is certainly an idea that should be considered by any potential franchisee.

Besides offering two or more complementary brands, such as pizza and frozen yogurt, in a single location, some enterprising franchisees combine a variety of franchised concepts to form a conglomerate of businesses. One business magazine, *INC* (November, 1998), cited an entrepreneur-franchisee who owned 21 Taco Bells, five Burger Kings, a KOA Campground, a Putt-Putt Golf & Games and a Country Inn & Suites by Carlson. The franchisee runs everything out of his office in Illinois and all franchise concepts share the same accounting and human resources staff. Each concept, however, has its own management staff. The owner says,

"I'm good at running a franchise, but I don't want to start from scratch ... franchises add credibility." Mega-franchisee business holdings are already proliferating and I expect that this type of ownership will only increase in the 21st century.

FRANCHISING FORMATS

Unless you've been living on another planet, you probably are already somewhat familiar with franchising. You may even patronize a variety of franchised businesses without realizing that they are franchises. These businesses run the gamut from car servicing and financial services to yogurt and voice mail. According to the International Franchise Association (IFA), franchised businesses are responsible for about one-third of all retail sales in the United States and a predicted 50% of all sales by the year 2000. Franchising is difficult to escape.

However, you may not know that there are two types of franchises: product and trade name franchises and business format franchises. In the former, the franchisee has use of a product or trade name, but no supporting relationship with the franchisor. This means that the franchisee basically operates the business independently, but does benefit from the marketing and advertising efforts of the franchise system. The products that are franchised are generally the older, established ones with a proven customer base. Product and trade name franchises are most commonly auto dealerships, gas stations and soft drink bottling companies. The business format franchise is the faster growing of the two and is the format we will discuss in this book. It is characterized by an on-going business relationship between franchisor and franchisee. The franchisee is offered not only a trademark and logo, but also a complete system of doing business. Business format franchises are famous around the world through companies such as McDonald's, Holiday Inn, Midas, Century 21 and Baskin-Robbins, to name a few.

In the best of all worlds, the business format franchise is mutually beneficial for franchisor and franchisee alike. The franchisee, by paying an initial fee, and, generally, an on-going royalty, gives the franchise system a continuous supply of working capital to develop and expand the organization. In turn, the franchisee gets a business package which would take years to develop and refine, a strengthened ability to compete through the established brand identity and marketing power of the system, and the cost benefits and clout associated with the franchisor's collective purchasing power.

"Buying" a Franchise

Now that you're excited about franchise opportunities, I'm going to tell you something that may disappoint you: You cannot "buy" a franchise. In actuality, you are engaging in a "leasing" transaction. Why is it a lease? In any franchise deal, the franchisee receives the assets up front, but only for a period of time—the term of the franchise agreement. The term of the agreement may run five or ten years or, in some cases, only one or two. Renewals of these agreements are at the option of the franchisor, and the reasons for not renewing an agreement should be completely spelled out in the Uniform Franchise Offering Circular (UFOC) and franchise agreement (see Chapter 5).

The fact that you are leasing and not purchasing a franchise may not influence your decision to become a franchisee, but this distinction must be kept in mind during the analytical, negotiating and agreement processes.

There are other important considerations as well. First, you must determine if you would function well as a franchisee. If so, you then have to choose the right franchise among the 2,500+ franchise opportunities available. That's only the beginning. After you whittle your franchise choices down to, maybe, a half dozen, you must then thoroughly investigate each opportunity. Once the choice is made, your job is to analyze and understand the franchise agreement and, if possible, negotiate points of disagreement or potential misunderstanding with the franchisor. Finally, you will have to put together a financial package to fund your franchise investment. The rest of this book is dedicated to exploring these issues and giving you the facts and practical knowledge that will result in a satisfying franchise selection.

2
WHAT MAKES A GOOD FRANCHISEE?

Enjoying what I'm doing is the prime motivation,
not money and not independence. None of
these is as important as the pure enjoyment of
liking what you're doing.
    BARRY ROBERTS
    Executrain franchisee

In an attempt to define the profile of the "average franchisee," *Franchise Times* conducted an extensive survey which was published, in part, in the August, 1997 issue. Their portrait of the average franchisee is as follows:

> A 48-year old male, owner of 3.5 units, working 52 hours a week, and, most likely, having attended or graduated from college.

This is somewhat misleading since we find that the franchisee population is being drawn from all walks of life. For example, today's franchisees include young people just out of college and women—both at an increasingly dramatic level. Whether or not you fit the survey's image of the average franchisee, let's look at how the franchisor evaluates potential franchisees and how you can decide if franchising is right for you.

THE QUALIFYING PROCESS

The majority of well-managed franchise systems do thorough background checks on potential franchisees. The typical screening process analyzes an applicant's resources, experience and character. (See the sample qualifying questionnaire at the end of this chapter.)

Most likely, the first qualification considered and investigated will be the prospect's financial situation. A qualifying questionnaire will include the following information:

- ❧ Assets—which include cash, home market value, savings funds, other real estate, stocks, bonds, securities, insurance (cash value), automobiles, your own business, notes receivable and other assets.

- ❧ Liabilities—which include loans and notes payable, charge accounts, real estate mortgages, loans against life insurance and other indebtedness.

- ❧ Net Worth—total assets less total liabilities.

- ❧ Sources of Income—which include salaries, bonuses and commissions, dividends and interest, real estate income and other sources.

This same qualifying questionnaire will ask questions about your educational history and previous employment. Often you are asked to supply names of credit references and personal references.

Many franchisors also ask questions in order to determine the candidate's motivation for buying a franchise, as well as to find out more about his or her personal characteristics. You can expect questions such as: Why are you interested in becoming associated with XYZ franchise? Why do you think you would be successful in an XYZ franchise? What are your goals for the next three years?

In order to ensure that the applicant has a clear understanding of both franchisee and franchisor responsibilities, franchisors have been asking questions such as: Why do franchisees pay an initial franchise fee? Why do franchisees pay an on-going franchise fee?

If you "pass" the first questionnaire and are asked to come to the corporate or regional headquarters for further discussions, you can expect additional questions of this kind and may even be given a "personality quiz" to see if you have the right temperament to run the franchise successfully.

Tip

On your first visit to corporate headquarters, you're not the only one being appraised. This is the time for you to evaluate the franchise management, both in style and in substance.

THE IDEAL FRANCHISEE

At the initial writing of this book in 1994, a franchisee that I interviewed explained: "A good candidate for a franchise is a person who has worked hard at a previous position. Someone who is 'dead wood' in a job will fail at a franchise." It's true that the ability and willingness to work hard is a "must-have" quality in order to succeed as a franchisee. Unfortunately, hard work is only a part of the franchisee picture. Not everyone is a suitable candidate for a franchise. To me, franchisees represent the middle ground between "employees" and "entrepreneurs." The vast majority of the population falls into and will be most successful as an "employee." The true "entrepreneurs" are few and far between, with the unique combination of steely determination, high energy and, most of all, the creative vision to take an idea and bring it to a successful conclusion. They are the founders of companies that begin from nothing. Franchisees, on the other hand, take a tried and proven concept that a franchisor has developed and follow the established procedures to run the business. Franchisees must possess certain characteristics in order to be truly happy and successful.

Figure 2.1 Assessment Worksheet

Do you have the necessary qualities to succeed as a franchisee? Answering and then scoring the following questions will get you into the right mind set to begin the introspective exercise of determining whether a franchise is right for you.

Questions
Answer all questions below with an "a," "b" or "c" response.

1. I need to control everything and like to make all the decisions myself. How true is this statement for you?
    a. Partially true.
    b. Completely true.
    c. Completely untrue.

2. Are you able to handle the day-to-day operation of a franchise business, which often includes taking over the duties of an absent employee?
    a. Yes, definitely.
    b. Not sure, but I would give it a try.
    c. No, it would be too difficult.

3. How strong is your motivation and drive to achieve success?
    a. Extremely strong, nothing will stand in my way.
    b. Strong, but other things in life are also important.
    c. Success in business isn't one of my goals.

4. Do you equate buying a franchise with "buying a job?"
    a. No, not at all.
    b. Yes, in some ways, I'm tired of job interviews.
    c. Yes, definitely, I'm unemployed.

5. Are you prepared to work long hours to make the business succeed?
   a. Yes, as long as it takes.
   b. Maybe, if it doesn't interfere with my recreation time.
   c. No, life is too short to work so hard.

6. Are you able to work without supervision and a support staff?
   a. Yes, definitely.
   b. I would give it a try, but I work better with a structured staff.
   c. No, I'm too used to working with a boss and other staff.

7. Are you able to organize your time and set priorities?
   a. Yes, I almost always do "first things first" and then go through the rest of the tasks.
   b. Yes, except if things get too hectic, then I seem to fall apart.
   c. Yes, but I don't like to plan ahead so sometimes things are done on time and sometimes they aren't.

8. Have you had five years or more of managerial or teaching experience?
   a. Yes.
   b. Less than five years' experience.
   c. No, never had managerial or teaching experience.

9. Have you ever hired and fired employees?
   a. Yes, I've done both without any problems.
   b. Yes, but I hate it, especially firing employees, so I tend to allow poor employees to stay on.
   c. No, it was never part of my job.

10. Have you ever trained personnel?
   a. Yes, and the majority of people worked out well and stay on the job.
   b. Yes, but it's not my favorite chore and many new hires leave.
   c. No.

11. How do you feel about performing a sales function?

a. I like making sales and like to convince people to buy my product or service.

b. I'm not crazy about making sales, but I know it's an important function.

c. I hate to make sales and would not expect to be involved in sales in any way.

12. Do you presently have sufficient capital (through personal funds or loans) to get through the start-up phase of a business?

a. Yes, I've been planning for it.

b. I don't have it now, but I have a pretty good idea where I can get it.

c. No, I hope to start making money immediately.

13. Franchisees often sign documents with investors, lending institutions, leasing companies and others. Are you mentally prepared for financial risk?

a. Yes, I understand and accept the risk.

b. Yes, but I would be shattered mentally and emotionally if I lost money.

c. No, I worked too hard for my money to put it at any kind of risk.

14. Is your spouse supportive of your starting a business?

a. Yes, very.

b. Don't know.

c. No, not at all.

15. Do you give up easily if things don't go as well as planned?

a. No, I am very persistent.

b. Sometimes I give up too easily, but other times I persist.

c. Yes, I go on to the next challenge.

Chapter 2

Scoring

Give yourself three points for every "a" answer, two points for every "b" answer and one point for every "c" answer. Total up all the points.

How Did You Score?

45–40 points: Good news! If you've been thinking seriously about owning a franchise, you have the basic qualities and experience to succeed.

39–33 points: Be very careful! Think through your responses to the questions and re-assess whether franchising will work for you.

32 points and below: Looks like trouble! Your responses indicate that either you won't be very happy or you won't be successful as a franchise owner.

After you have scored your answers, whatever the outcome, ask yourself if you have a strong desire to achieve. This is a common trait for success in both a franchise and an independent business.

Here is a checklist of questions which will further aid you in your self-analysis.

1. *Are you able to work within the structure of a franchise system?* With a franchise, you'll be buying into a proven business system with prescribed ways of operating. Many of the decisions have already been made for you. If you need to control everything or like to make all the decisions yourself, this could pose a problem.

2. *Are you "buying a job"?* Think carefully about your reasons for considering a franchise. If you have been unemployed or under-employed for some time, operating a franchise can seem like an enticing solution. Self-employment is not for everyone and it is certainly not a cure-all for joblessness.

3. *Are you prepared to work long hours in order to make the business succeed?* There's just no getting around it. Even with the assistance of the franchisor's staff, there will not be enough hours in the day to do everything. The first years as a franchisee will be especially stressful.

4. *Are you able to work without supervision and a support staff?* Although you will have the structure of the franchise system to fall back on, the day-to-day decisions will have to be made in a timely fashion. In all likelihood, you won't be getting significant input from any employees, so you will have to make the decisions alone. In addition, you'll probably have the job of choosing and placing advertising materials, as well as running the copy machine. You'll have to wear many hats.

5. *Are you mentally prepared for financial risk?* You'll be signing documents with investors, lending institutions, leasing companies and others. Although you will try to minimize your business risk by choosing wisely, financial risk is always present.

6. *Is your spouse supportive of your starting a business?* Whether the spouse works in the business or not, 100% support is a necessity if you want both the business and the marriage to succeed.

7. *Are you able to organize your time?* Since time is your most precious commodity, you must be able to strip away the non-essentials and prioritize the rest.

8. *Do you give up easily if things don't go as planned?* Any new business will have its peaks and valleys. You will have to be persistent about reaching your goals and look at momentary setbacks as just part of the process.

Tip

Don't be upset if the result of your self-appraisal is not encouraging for franchising. After all, the objective of the analysis is not to buy a franchise, but to avoid making a costly mistake.

From the Franchisor's Viewpoint

To be sure, possessing all the following qualities of the ideal franchisee is rare, but most franchisors look for the following characteristics in their franchisees:

- ➤ A person with strong motivation and the drive to achieve success.

- ➤ A person with confidence and enthusiasm for the product or service being sold, rather than just a desire to make a profit.

- ➤ A person who does *not* have all the administrative and entrepreneurial skills necessary to start, develop and operate a viable business, and who, therefore, needs the franchisor's support (a front-line supervisor or middle manager would be a good choice rather than someone who is a self-starter and has already founded a business).

- ➤ A person who is not only good at learning new things, but who is also able to motivate and train others.

- ➤ A person with at least five years of managerial or teaching experience.

- ➤ A person who has experience in, or a good working knowledge of, the industry in which the franchisor does business.

A few industries, most notably some fast-food systems, do not seek the last qualification. Several fast-food systems automatically disqualify applicants with a restaurant background. The idea here is that a franchisee freshly trained in the franchisor's procedures will be more successful than one coming from the same industry with different and often conflicting habits.

Similarly, many hair and beauty salon franchises will not recruit technical people (such as hair stylists and cosmetologists). Instead, they look to business people with no hair styling or beauty skills to become franchisees. The franchisors believe that management skills, attention to customer service and sales skills are the most important qualifications.

Many franchisees already operating in a system have opinions as to how prospective franchisees should be evaluated. After all, they have an investment to protect. A Taco John's franchisee had the following to say: "I would look for a franchisee who would positively benefit the chain. The franchisor shouldn't just pocket the $20,000 fee and in two years watch the franchisee fail. They should look for people who are dedicated and have enough resources to be successful. Basically, they should be more discriminating about whom they enlist. The ultimate success of the franchise lies in the strength of the franchisees."

Tip

In order to qualify, some systems, such as McDonald's and Domino's, require that the prospective franchisee works as an employee in a pilot program before buying the franchise. Though time-consuming and arduous, this technique nearly eliminates the risk of failure as a franchisee.

From the Franchisee's Viewpoint

When I asked franchisees, "What makes a good franchisee?", they gave one overwhelming answer—*a good salesperson*. Just about every franchisee—

from businesses as diverse as management training to high-tech printing to residential cleaning to check cashing—mentioned sales skills as a prime requisite.

Quite a few people also expressed surprise at the amount of time taken up by the sales and marketing duties. Those franchisees who had no experience in sales were at a distinct disadvantage and had to learn in a hurry or else lose the businesses.

Tip

If you have no experience with sales and don't care to learn, you'd better think twice about buying a franchise.

As an adjunct to the emphasis on sales, franchise owners need a healthy self-image to handle all the rejections that come their way. It is important, however, not to take every rejection as a personal affront. The most successful franchisees look at the sales function as a numbers game, where, if they persist in their efforts, they will ultimately reach their goals.

In addition to a strong sales orientation, a successful franchisee must have a high energy level. Almost all the franchisees talk about the long hours, 80 hours a week in some cases. The bigger frustration, however, is in not receiving a salary commensurate with the amount of time and effort. A franchisee can expect a slim salary for a tremendous amount of work, at least for the first year or two of operations. So, in addition to a high energy level, a certain resiliency is also necessary.

SHOULD YOU START YOUR OWN BUSINESS?

Owning your own business has always been a part of the American Dream. With the advent of franchising, however, you now have a choice between starting your own independent business or operating your own business unit as part of a franchise system. This choice will usually hinge upon the type of business that interests you, your personality, your finances and your risk-quotient.

But first, let's look at some general statistics. It is estimated that there are more than 550,000 franchise businesses in the U.S. today, generating more than $800 billion in annual sales. Precise success rates for independent businesses versus franchised ones are not available, but most business experts believe that franchised businesses have a better chance of success than independently-owned small businesses. The numbers published by the Department of Commerce and the U.S. Small Business Administration come the closest to offering a valid comparison. The Department of Commerce reported that, since 1971, less than 5% of franchised businesses have failed or been discontinued each year. (This does not account for franchised businesses that may have been transferred to a new owner.) On the other side, the U.S. Small Business Administration reports that 65% of business start-ups fail within five years.

When it comes to making a decision between opening an independent business or buying into a franchise system, the statistics can tell you only so much. To make the right decision, you'll have to take stock of your personality, working style, access to financing and risk sensitivity.

Interestingly enough, the majority of both franchisees and independent business people share one quality. They value independence over security. Where they differ the most is in their risk threshold and their tolerance for bureaucracy. The true entrepreneur will be willing to live with risk (sometimes extreme) if the projected payoff is sufficient and will have a very low tolerance for controls and procedures. The "ideal franchisee," however, is somewhat risk-adverse and is willing to pay the price (the franchise fee and royalties) to diminish the overall risk of failure. This franchisee will also faithfully follow controls and procedures. After all, the system is part of the purchase price, and strict adherence to its tenets promises success.

The entrepreneur—the type most likely to succeed as an independent businessperson—will sometimes find her or his application rejected by the franchisor. Since conformity to the franchisor's format and operating dictums are critical for success, the franchisor will reject anyone who seems to show resistance to standard operating procedures. Franchisors also believe that entrepreneurs may be openly critical of things they don't like, may lose interest in the routine tasks of running the franchise, and may quickly start to look for the next challenge.

Tip

Don't count yourself out if you have a true entrepreneurial personality. Large area developing, multi-unit franchising and international franchising can be perfect for the entrepreneur. These franchise formats provide constant new challenges and a degree of control almost equal to that of the franchisor.

FRANCHISEES WHO HAVE BEEN THERE

Many of the franchisees we talked with had to make a decision first on whether they would open an independent business or a franchised one. A few of their stories follow.

Before a New Jersey man decided to buy a fast-food franchise, he asked himself this question: "How comfortable do I feel about going into the unknown?" He answered, "Not very." Although he was familiar with engineering, manufacturing and construction work, he knew very little about the food business. Even so, he purchased a snack foods business. Now, after nearly ten years of operation, he is ready to give up on the franchise. His current goal is to open and operate five independent stores that carry similar products. Not only has the ownership of the franchise system changed several times, but he believes that "the franchise system squashes the creativeness of the individual. You can be prohibited from bringing anything new into the system."

Barry Pasarew is a Voice-Tel franchisee in the high-tech voice message business. The business utilizes sophisticated equipment and elaborate service networks. Pasarew says, "It would be close to impossible to do this business on your own because of the necessity of a network. The franchise system allows you to get started immediately. It saves dollars and time so you can focus on selling and developing."

Jim Gendreau owns an independent distribution company, but he was still drawn to franchising. He owns multiple units of the Cost Cutters franchise in the hair salon business. When asked why he didn't start the business independently, especially since he was an experienced businessperson, he said, "The big difference between an independent and a franchise is the marketing and advertising clout and expertise the franchise brings. Secondly, all the bugs are out of the system by the time you buy it."

Linda Moore, a Ledger Plus franchisee, considered both an independent and a franchise business after leaving a position in a large corporation. She says, "Unless you have a very unique business idea, it's almost foolish not to buy a franchise. Success rates are not as good for independents. Most people have skills in one or two areas, but with a franchise, you can get help in areas outside your expertise."

Ken Wisotzky had an independent ice cream store prior to owning a Gloria Jean's and a My Favorite Muffin. The ice cream business was going well, so why didn't he continue? Wisotzky says, "The mall developer wouldn't renew the lease on my store. They wanted a 'name-brand' tenant." According to him, many developers, realtors and landlords consider franchises stronger tenants, and so the franchisee can get better space.

Bernie Wolff ran an independent photography studio in Florida before he took on two franchised units with Glamour Shots. Even though his day-to-day responsibilities have only changed slightly, he's happy he made the change. He says his old business had monthly sales from $16,000 to $18,000. When he switched to the Glamour Shots franchise in 1992, his monthly average for the first four months was $38,000 to $40,000. He attributes the increase to the impact of the franchise name.

When faced with making a decision on buying a mobile laundry and dry-cleaning franchise, Patrick McClune's wife and friends advised him to "do it himself." They told him, "You're smart and resourceful and you shouldn't pay for a logo that's not very well known." McClune asked the franchise system what he was getting that was proprietary. They said that he would receive training, the system for doing business and the logo. So, McClune went with the franchise and now concludes that the franchise did give him a "jump-start" and a good system for conducting business.

Tip

Sometimes the choice between independent and franchise depends on the type of business. A publishing business franchisee told me, "Fast-food, for example, needs a name company. A franchise works best. Publishing, on the other hand, is a business you may be able to do independently. For example, I have a competitor that is an independent business, and it does at least as well as we do."

MAJOR FRANCHISEE POOLS

Who will be the owners of franchises as we move into the 21st century? According to Don DeBolt, President of the International Franchise Association, "The new pool of franchisees will resemble the heartland of the current franchise mix." Just like the current pool, it will, most likely, include men and women who desire a career change, are fed up with corporate life, dream of owning their own business, want a second or third career, or have converted their independent business to a franchise.

Mr. DeBolt believes all these reasons and objectives for becoming a franchisee will still hold true for franchisees in the near future. However, he does envision changes in the mix of individuals who will seek franchising as the solution to owning their own business. He believes a greater percentage of women and minorities will enter franchising in the future. More and more franchise systems are exploring and implementing strategies for recruiting women and minorities in order to take advantage of this trend. Importantly, Mr. DeBolt says, "Young people—under 30—will be increasingly attracted to franchising." This segment sees franchising as a successful business strategy. Franchising is especially appealing to those young people who want to take control of their lives and careers. Also, retirees and ex-military personnel will increasingly choose franchising, not for "money to live on," but as a way to diversify an investment portfolio and engage in a meaningful activity. Lastly, ex-corporate workers will continue as an important part of the franchisee pool, although to a lesser extent than four or five years ago when all the corporate downsizing occurred.

Let's examine some of the franchise pool—ex-corporate workers, women, minorities, young people and retired military. Do they have the general characteristics that are essential to be successful as a franchisee?

The Corporate Dropout

The corporate dropout has several advantages. Many corporate workers are accustomed to *systems*. As this is exactly what you're buying with a franchise, these workers immediately feel a degree of comfort and familiarity. Their expertise and experience are also often transferable to a franchise. For example, many have experience in sales and marketing, which is a real asset for almost all types of franchises. If they were line managers, they have a financial background, which is invaluable in businesses where cash flow is critical. Then, also, they tend to be computer literate, which gives them an edge using the software programs the franchisor provides for administrative and accounting purposes. All these skills can help the ex-corporate worker get off to a faster start than the average franchisee.

This corporate experience edge is illustrated by Rich Habel, a Mail Boxes, Etc. franchisee in Washington, DC. He previously worked for a major corporation where his self-discipline and customer service skills helped him succeed. He's found these abilities equally important and applicable to his shipping business.

In some instances, however, corporate experience can work against you. For example, some franchise systems don't look upon ex-corporate workers as ideal candidates and may even reject their applications. Some of the reasons given for rejection are:

- Ex-corporate workers are not used to functioning without a support staff. Unlike the corporate world, the boss must wear a lot of hats since there are fewer employees.

- They do not pay attention to bottom line figures and lack a profit orientation. Often previous corporate experience simply dictates that the person operate "within the budget."

- They are not psychologically suited to the rough-and-tumble world of franchising after the somewhat sheltered and structured corporate environment.

- They lack entrepreneurial spirit. They not only need a willingness to follow the system, but also a high energy level and a drive to excel.

Although few franchise systems will actually reject an enthusiastic and financially qualified ex-corporate worker, there is no doubt that some of these perceptions will surface in the first meeting with the franchisor. They are valid assessments of some ex-corporate people, and you need to think carefully about whether they apply to you. After all, the purpose of all the discussions and appraisals is to avoid making a mistake which can prove to be both financially and personally devastating.

A large number of ex-corporate people, however, are succeeding very well in spite of some franchisors' apprehensions. Fred Banty, a Padgett Business Service franchisee, has some ideas on why this is true. He says, "For an ex-corporate person, a franchise is like having a network and support around you [as in a corporation]. It's not as scary or risky as an independent business. Franchises push you to market the product or service, give you a standard operating procedure, and will take up the slack for insufficient entrepreneurial skills."

Tip

Be realistic and patient. *Ex-corporate workers must realize that they will be going from a predictable weekly income to next to nothing for the first year or more. It could take as long as several years for a reliable income will follow. The saving grace: the potential for a large income is better at your own business than as a corporate employee.*

As we enter the 21st Century, an interesting trend is emerging in a variety of franchise systems. Although some of the personality traits and experiences of a corporate worker don't always lend themselves to a single-unit franchise, a multi-unit franchise may work perfectly!

What accounts for this? It seems that as the franchisee acquires additional units, the job evolves from that of a worker/manager to that of a CEO. This is when organizational and communication skills come into play, and when executive capabilities become an important ingredient in the success of the multi-unit system.

Tip

If the slow and tedious pace of a corporate job is a major reason for you to leave, operating a franchise should be a good choice. If, however, you want to leave the corporation because of stress and long hours, don't buy a franchise. Most franchisees work 60–85 hours a week, at least in the beginning, and stress is almost always present.

Women

The U.S. Department of Commerce reports that women are opening businesses twice as fast as men, and many of these women are taking a hard look at franchising. Most of these prospective owners fall into one of two camps. Either they are corporate workers looking for a faster track in private enterprise, having hit the "glass ceiling," or they are complete novices who believe they can "buy" the necessary business acumen by signing on with a franchisor. They expect the franchisor to teach them how to operate and manage a profitable business.

Other women are drawn to franchising because of the flexibility and personal freedom of running their own businesses. In spite of all the hard work and long hours, owning a business often makes juggling home, children and career a possibility.

Although women who are ex-corporate workers will have to confront the negative perceptions of some franchisors, most franchisors believe women can be good franchisees, and, in fact, many aggressively seek women owners. Many women with corporate experience are opting for business service franchises, such as leadership training, motivational seminars, accounting services and the like.

Sandi Vettle and Grace Thompson, both coming out of large corporations, are Leadership Management franchisees. When asked why she chose a franchise business, Vettle said, "I didn't want to have to reinvent the wheel. I also needed some good programming tools and especially the psychological support." Thompson's explanation is that "the quality of the materials [from the franchisor] is so excellent and professionally done that it would be difficult to duplicate independently. The investment of time and energy to try and do it yourself just isn't worth it."

Many franchisors say women make good franchisees because they excel at team building and cooperative efforts, both of which are foundations of the franchise system. Franchisors also note that women seem to be more enthusiastic about the support and structure inherent in a franchise system. "Attention to detail" is also mentioned as a quality that is a real plus in women franchisees. For example, several of the women who own fast-food franchises showed their immaculate restrooms, an area that often falls by the wayside in this fast-paced industry. Not so for these owners who made cleanliness a top priority. The franchise systems, in their frequent unannounced inspections, notice the difference and give women owners/co-owners high marks.

Some franchise systems, such as Decorating Den and A Choice Nanny, sell nearly all their units to women. Other businesses that traditionally attract women are the retail, health and beauty and cleaning services sectors. But more and more women are moving into less traditional areas. For example, women are seen in increasing numbers in businesses such as automotive services, security systems and restaurants.

A Nontraditional Franchisee. Paula Ford is a sub-franchisee of Dent Doctor, a paintless dent removal business. Her brother-in-law, Ray Chappell, is the master franchisee for a large territory in Texas and Oklahoma. Paula works a portion of the territory, paying a percentage of her sales to Ray as a sub-franchisee (the company calls her an "associate").

Having left a corporate secretarial position because she "was fed up with it," Paula admits that giving up a regular paycheck was a little scary for her. She considered looking for another job, but found her job opportunities very limited. It was then that the idea of joining her brother-in-law in the dent removal business came to her.

After attending a bare minimum of training (three weeks at the corporate center), Paula continued with another five weeks of hands-on training with Ray. Even so, the work was so painstaking and difficult that, in the beginning, she was only able to work on small hail damage. She couldn't work very fast or on very big dents. Now, though, after only a year on the job, all that has changed, and her productivity has increased greatly.

Best of all, Paula finds that she is really happy with what she is doing. She loves the independence and making her own hours. Paula recalls, "The most negative thing about being a secretary was that, if something went wrong, it was your fault, whether you had control of it or not. On the other hand, you didn't get recognized if things went well." Now Paula gets direct feedback from her customers, and she loves it when they praise her for a good job.

How does the rest of the world look at a woman knocking out car dents? Paula says there has been little reaction from the customers—as long as she gets the job done. She admits that as a physically small woman, there are some larger dents she won't take on because of the sheer physical force needed to repair them.

As to whether she would make the same choice one year later, the answer is definitely "yes." Since the business is almost all labor, with very little overhead, she started making a profit from the beginning. In fact, says Paula, "The first week out of training, I made what it would have taken me a month to do in my previous job."

Reaching Out to Minorities

Franchise systems across the country are instituting special advertising campaigns, training programs, support systems and financial programs to recruit and retain minority franchisees. Denny's, for example, settled a much publicized class-action lawsuit in 1995 alleging minority discrimination in the system, and now has an estimated 27% (194) of its 720 franchised restaurants owned by minorities. For the most part, "minorities" are specifically African-Americans, Hispanics, Asians and Native Americans.

The Minorities in Franchising Committee of the International Franchise Association (IFA) has conceived a new program, the Franchise Trade Delegation Program (FTD). The FTD will facilitate the process of linking franchisors with prospective minority franchisees. In addition to the franchisors, financial intermediaries, community-based organizations and state and federal government agencies will be involved in the collective effort. Write the International Franchise Association at 1350 New York Ave., NW, # 900, Washington, DC 20005, or call at (202) 628-8000, for more information.

Franchisors that actively recruit minorities usually want these franchisees to operate in inner cities and to deal with customers from a similar ethnic background. Although fast-food operations and restaurants have been the most active in promoting these programs, other franchise systems with a variety of businesses are coming up with special minority franchise opportunities.

A sampling of the minority franchise programs follow:

- In order to boost franchise ownership by minorities, Burger King has a "Memorandum of Understanding" with the U.S. Department of Commerce's Minority Business Development Agency (MBDA), which is designed to assist minorities in identifying franchise and supply opportunities in the Burger King system, and will also aid minorities in identifying viable sources of financing.

- The Cendant Corporation, franchisor of such hotel brands as Days Inn, Ramada Inn, Travelodge, Howard Johnson and Knights Inn, has a special financing program for qualified African-American and Hispanic franchisees. The financing provides the franchisee with a development advance equal to $1,000 per guest room for facilities with up to 75 rooms and $1,500 per guest room for those over 75 guest rooms, with a maximum of $150,000. Cendant and Cendant Finance Holding Corporation have put aside $5 million to fund such financing. The development advance is not subject to repayment unless the franchisee terminates before 15 years of operation, or if the facility transfers.

The following franchise companies have developed minority programs (as per the National Minority Franchising Initiative):

Accor Economy Lodging
14643 Dallas Pkwy., # 870
Dallas, TX 75254
Ms. Cynthia Gartman
(972) 702-5963

Allied Domecq
15 Pacella Park Dr.
Randolph, MA 02368
Mr. Tony Padulo
(773) 695-8849

Cendant Corporation
1 Sylvan Way
Parsippany, NJ 07054
Mr. David Hardy
(973) 496-7439

Express Personnel
6300 NW Expressway
Oklahoma City, OK 73132
Mr. Jeffrey C. Bevis
(877) 652-6400 (405) 840-5000

Jani-King
16885 Dallas Pkwy.
Addison, TX 75001
Mr. Chuck Gibson
800/552-5264 972/991-0900

Metromedia Restaurant Group
6500 International Pkwy., # 1000
Plano, TX 75093-8222
Ms. Lynette McKee
(800) 543-9670 (407) 333-3533

PostNet Postal & Business Centers
181 N. Arroya Grande Blvd., # 100 A
Henderson, NV 89014-1625

Mr. Brian Spindel
(800) 841-7171

Servicemaster
860 Ridge Lake Blvd., C2-1834
Memphis, TN 38120-9417
Mr. David Messenger
(800) 633-5703

Sign-A-Rama
1801 Australian Ave. South
West Palm Beach, FL 33409
Mr. Kevin Wheeler
(561) 640-5570

Six Continents Hotels
3 Ravinia Dr., # 2900
Atlanta, GA 30346
Mr. Brown Kessler
(770) 604-2107

Subway Restaurants
325 Bic Dr.
Milford, CT 06460-3059
Ms. Lisa Palmieri
(800) 888-4848 (203) 877-4281
www.subway.com

The Athlete's Foot
1950 Vaughn Rd.
Kennesaw, GA 30144
Mr. Martin Amschler
(800) 524-6444 (770) 514-4676

WingStop Restaurants
1234 Northwest Hwy.
Garland, TX 75041-5834
Mr. Bruce Evans
(972) 686-6500

Yorkshire Global Restaurants   Mr. Bryon Stephens
P.O. Box 11988, 101 Yorkshire Blvd.   (800) 545-8360 (859) 543-6000
Lexington, KY 40579-1988

Young People

One of the biggest changes in the make-up of the franchisee population, since the first publication of this book in 1994, is the now very visible segment of young people. This new generation of twenty and thirtysome-things is highly involved in franchising—both as franchisors and franchisees. This book's subject is not to dwell on franchisors, but, suffice it to say, that some of the most exciting franchise concepts in the last few years have been introduced by individuals in their 20s.

According to current research, 20–34-year olds are going into business for themselves three times as frequently as 35–55-year olds. This younger population is attracted to franchising as a means of operating their own business.

In some cases, she or he first works in a franchise system as a franchisee and, after seeing the merits of a franchised business, then buys her or his own license. This was the case with Tim and Tania Oldfield, both native Australians in their late 20s, who have purchased the rights to develop 50 Cash Converter stores in the state of Virginia by 2004. Tim Oldfield has no qualms about meeting this goal and believes that his stint at a fast-food franchise in Australia and the UK called Country Fried Chicken helped prepare him to be a franchise area developer. "It usually helps to have experience on both sides of the fence," says Oldfield. Oldfield chose franchising (even though he possesses a degree in economics) because he doesn't enjoy "being stuck in an office" and is very "people-oriented."

The Oldfields, as of this writing, had only opened their first store seven weeks earlier. Cash Converters is a retail resale store of all kinds of goods, including musical instruments and computers. Both Tim and Tania work about 65–70 hours weekly in the store now, but, as soon as a good store manager is hired, they will concentrate more on managing this store and developing the others.

Terry Spicer, the youngest franchisee at Mrs. Fields Cookies system, says, "I worked twice as hard to prove to the Mrs. Fields Cookie Corporation that I could run and operate my own business despite my age." Apparently he is succeeding. In 1995 Spicer, purchased a company-owned store, opened a second unit a year later, and opened his third unit in February, 1998.

Often the franchises are opened by young husband and wife partners, as the Oldfields and others like Don Morello and his wife Jean, both in their early 30s, who are Cousins Subs franchisees. The couple was able to complete a ten-store Cousins Subs development agreement in only two years in Beloit, WI. They more recently purchased the development rights to Dane County, WI from the company. They are not only ambitious; they are also innovative. For example, they take the unique approach of giving the existing managers of their stores the opportunity to purchase a minority ownership in the store after three years.

Retired Military

Across the board, franchisors are targeting ex-military personnel, a formidable pool that is continuing to grow as potential franchisees. There are an estimated 30 million veterans in the United States, and 275,000 more leave the Armed Services each year.

Franchisors agree that experience with the military system translates to a healthy respect for and adherence to a franchise system's way of doing business. They find that military people respect the value of training, are enthusiastic learners and follow orders. As an added plus, many ex-military are trained in sophisticated technological systems, enabling them to quickly learn computer systems and technology-based businesses.

Often, experiences gained in the military can be transferred into a successful franchise career. Ex-military people should look at the type of training and experience they've had in the Armed Forces, and then choose a franchise system which capitalizes on this. The teamwork and discipline learned in the military will be invaluable in the process of operating the franchise and dealing with employees.

Many, if not most, franchise systems are welcoming ex-military into their ranks. Following are a few of the systems that make a real effort to recruit from the military:

- HouseMaster, Bound Brook, NJ—makes inspections on homes before real-estate closings to make sure homes are structurally sound.

- Relax the Back Corporation, El Segundo, CA—retail stores that sell products designed to help back pain.

- A&W Restaurants, Inc., Livonia, MI—one of the oldest franchise systems, serving its famous root beer, hamburgers and hot dogs.

- Rainbow International Carpet, Dyeing and Cleaning Co., Waco, TX—service company for carpet, upholstery, drapery and ceiling cleaning, restoration, etc.

FINAL WORDS

The first step in our exploration of franchise opportunities is a self-analysis. Think carefully about whether you have the necessary traits to succeed—traits such as a strong desire to achieve, a high energy level, persistence in reaching a goal, self-motivation and a strong sales orientation. Be brutally honest in your appraisal and only continue the franchise search if your temperament and personality fit the bill.

Figure 2.2 Sample Qualifying Questionnaire

Personal Data and Business History

Name:_____Age:_____

Address:_____# Years in Area:_____

City:_____State:_____Zip:_____

Social Security #:_____Date of Birth:_____

Dependents:_____Ages:_____

Spouse's First Name:_____

Spouse's Occupation:_____

Home Phone:(___)_____Business Phone:(___)_____

Business Address:_____

Other Business Connections (Officer, Director, Owners, Partners, etc.):

_____

_____

_____

_____

Business Experience

From	To	Firm	Position	Annual Income

Exact Nature of Business Experience (including self-employment):

_____

_____

_____

_____

Do you now own any franchise? (Describe.):_____

_____

_____

Have you ever failed in business or compromised with creditors? If you have: when, where, circumstances (including any remaining liabilities):

_____

_____

_____

Education	Degree/Level Attained	Year Graduated
1.		
2.		
3.		

Military	Dates	Rank
1.		
2.		
3.		

How is your health?_____U.S. Citizen?_____
What professional magazines and trade journals do you read?

_____

Do you own any patents or copyrights?_____
Hobbies?_____

Business References

Individual	Title	Company	City	Phone
1.				
2.				
3.				

Character References

Name	Address	Phone
1.		
2.		
3.		

Memberships (Civic, Business, Professional):_____
_____
_____

Financial Data

Your Personal Bank:_____

Contact:_____Phone:_____

Address:_____City:_____

Assets	Total
Cash	
Securities—Readily Negotiable	
Real Estate—Fair Market Value, Residence	
Real Estate—Fair Market Value, Other	
Notes Receivable	
Business Ventures—Liquid	
Business Ventures—Non-Liquid	
Life Insurance	
Retirement Fund	
Income Tax Fund	
All Other Assets	
Total Assets	$

Liabilities	Monthly Payment	Total
Mortgages 1st Residence		
Mortgages 2nd Residence		
Mortgages—Other		
Lines of Credit		
Vehicle/Boat Loans		
Credit Card and All Other Liabilities		
Total Liabilities		$
Net Worth		$

How do you propose to fund this investment?

_____

_____

_____

_____

_____

_____

Management Plans

If you were approved, when could you begin training?_____

Territories in which you are interested? (1st Choice):_____

(2nd Choice):_____

Are there any investor-associates who would join you in this venture (Please have each fill out one of these forms.)

Names:_____

_____

_____

Comments

Please use this space to tell us anything else you think is relevant, i.e. your present business objectives, and as I consider my experiences and abilities, I am confident that I can operate a successful franchise primarily because:

_____

_____

_____

_____

_____

_____

_____

_____

To the best of my knowledge and ability the information I have submitted is correct.

_____   _____

Signature   **Date**

3
CHOOSING THE RIGHT FRANCHISE

Every morning when I get up, I am just tingling to get to this place [his IHOP restaurant].
   An IHOP franchisee since 1972

Why work the long hours only to walk away with $40,000 a year, if you are lucky? This restaurant is open 363 days a year, 16 hours a day. It is too much.
   An IHOP franchisee since 1990

In this chapter and the next, I'm going to tell you how to *choose the right franchise*. Remember, this is not an easy task with over 2,500 franchise systems to choose from. But, however painstaking and time-consuming the process becomes, it's worth it! I am convinced that if you choose a franchise wisely, your chances of success are almost assured.

SETTING PRIORITIES

If you remember one thing from this book, it should be this: before making any decision on a franchise, sit down, analyze your needs, capabilities and limitations in relation to a franchise business. This could take as little as a few days or as much as several years. In either case, it is the most important step, so don't skip it.

Let's say you have looked at independent businesses and franchises and have definitely decided that a franchise business is for you. Your next step is to carefully answer questions like the following:

- Where will the business be located? In the city, the suburbs, the countryside? Do I want to commute? If so, what are the time limits? 30 minutes? 60 minutes?
- Do I want a home-based business?
- Do I want to work five days a week? Six or seven?
- Do I want to be an absentee owner?
- Is there a specific industry I want to work in?

These questions and other critical ones can be found in the worksheet in Figure 3.1. I encourage you to complete it before looking at specific franchises. Once you have completed the worksheet, determine which factors are non-negotiable and which are negotiable. In this way, you will set up a list of priorities that will guide you through the decision-making process.

DECIDING ON BASICS

An important choice that you will have to make, either as part of your priorities list or later when you've zeroed in on a particular industry or business, is the choice between a large, established franchise system and a small, newer one, or something in between. This is a critical decision, because the age and size of the system will impact you in many ways.

Trap

Be careful if your choice is a very small or a very large franchise system. If there are only a few operating units, the franchisor may not have enough experience to make it work, and if the system is very large, all the regions may be saturated and you'll have to settle for less than prime locations.

Figure 3.1 Worksheet for Setting Priorities

Answering these questions will give you a good start toward setting priorities for a franchise choice.

1. Where will the business be located? In the city, the suburbs, the countryside?

2. Do I want to commute? If so, what are the time limits?

3. Do I want a home-based business?

4. Do I want to work five days a week? Six or seven? How many hours per day?

5. Do I want to be an absentee owner?

6. Is there a specific industry I want to work in?

7. Are there any industries, products or services that I will not work with under any circumstances?

8. Are there any specific characteristics that must exist in the business?

9. Do I want a product or service franchise?

10. Do I want a new or an established system?

11. Do I want a large or small franchise system?

12. Do I want a system with slow and steady growth or a rapid growth one?

13. What kind of attitude do I want from the franchisor? Paternalistic? Dictatorial? Collegial? Laid back?

14. How important is name recognition? On a regional or national basis?

15. Will I be happy with one or two franchised units or do I want to own multiple units or develop an entire area?

16. How much can I realistically invest in a franchise (money that does not have to be borrowed or raised elsewhere)?

17. How much should the total investment be?

18. Do I need to find a franchisor that offers a low-interest financing program or has an established third party financing relationship?

THE FRANCHISING SUPERSTARS

The highly visible, larger franchise systems, such as Choice Hotels, Dunkin' Donuts, Jiffy Lube, Pizza Hut and Century 21 Real Estate are well-capitalized and have a demonstrated track record and an experienced management staff. For the most part, they can be looked at as lower risk investments.

Since they have a greater number of franchisees, the new franchisee will accrue more co-operative benefits. This means a powerful advertising reach, better name and brand recognition, preferential treatment from suppliers and lower operating costs through volume purchasing.

Tip

One of the biggest reasons for choosing a known name franchise is instant customers.

But before you sign on the dotted line, also consider the downside of a big name franchise. For one, the larger, mature franchises tend to be in flat markets with many competitors. More important for new franchisees, there are often few good locations available. Then, too, participation in this lower risk opportunity usually means a very large entry cost, because the brand name is so strong—less risk means a higher entry fee.

On the operating side, these systems often become more authoritarian and bureaucratic as they grow. The corporation can get so enmeshed with administrative duties that it loses touch with its marketplace. Some franchisees feel lost in the shuffle while others have even the smallest decisions dictated to them by their franchisor. Some franchisees flourish with this type of control. When asked how the franchise operates, a happy casual restaurant owner replied, "We follow the franchisors' guidelines 100%. What they say, we do. They want everything to be very uniform and they tell us how much we should be using and how much we should be selling."

Several of the fast-food franchisees we talked to emphatically stated that you get both instant customers and nearly instant profits with a big name. But George Hayden, a Wendy's franchisee, says, "It still isn't for everybody. You must have the temperament to be able to deal with large bank debt to start the business." In addition, several franchisees mentioned the heavy degree of control exerted by the franchisor. One gave as an example a case where the fast-food restaurant needed a separate women's bathroom but the store size stipulated only one bathroom, so the franchisor refused to allow it.

One franchisee was critical of a large fast-food purveyor who only allows people who come up through their system to buy a franchise. Typically, the prospective franchisee comes out of college with no real business experience, and goes through the ranks, working at various jobs. The interviewed franchisee summed it up like this: "The system is looking for a pliable person only trained in the franchisor's way of doing business."

The Rising Stars

About 60% of all franchise companies have fewer than 50 locations, so you'll have a bigger choice if you opt for the newer, smaller systems. However, just as with the big name franchises, you will have a variety of negatives and positives to consider first.

One big feature is that the up-and-coming franchisor tends to be in an uncrowded industry that is not overrun with competitors. Ideally, the business is currently considered "hot," the franchisor has royalty fees, and it will negotiate the terms of the transaction. The system management is usually flexible, not set in its ways and encourages participation from the franchisees.

Tip

If you decide to be one of the first franchise operators for a new system, negotiate hard. Your risk is proportionately higher and you should be compensated for this.

These benefits, however, are offset by some costs. The newer franchise poses a somewhat higher risk than the established one. For one thing, there's no demonstrated track record. The franchisors may not have worked out all the bugs in the system, and you'll have to experiment right along with them. Then, too, a small number of franchisees undoubtedly brings less advertising power—with a corresponding lack of name recognition—and usually higher wholesale prices for the franchisee.

Trap

Investigate the capitalization of a new franchise very thoroughly. If the franchisor is not well capitalized, the entire program may collapse—and you along with it.

Once you have made a choice on the size of the franchise system, you might want to be even more specific. For example, if you prefer a smaller franchise system, you can set a minimum number of operating units to act as a guideline. You may limit your choice to systems that have, say, 20–100 units, or perhaps a mid-sized franchise with 150–400 units. Conversely, if you find the larger systems more appealing, then you may set limits of no less than 500 or more than 2,000 units.

You will undoubtedly find pros and cons with each size system. Here are some comments from franchisees of varying-sized systems that may help you zero in on what size will work best for you.

From franchisees of Papa John's, a large regional chain: "When Papa John's was a lot smaller, five or six years ago, they didn't give us much support. They do now and communication is much better. The franchisor is very supportive and franchisees get memos which discuss where we are ranked in our region and other important information. With growth, things have gotten better for the franchisees."

From franchisees of another regional chain, Taco John's, which, like many regional franchises or smaller franchises, worry about brand strength: "The product name is only strong where there are a lot of Taco John's. Taco John's has been around 20 years, but we are still a small company. There are not enough stores for name recognition." (In spite of this worry, however, most franchisees of this system were happy.)

From a fast-food franchisee of a large system that has been going through some image re-vamping as a result of decreasing sales: "We've been franchisees for 14 years with two stores. Pretty much we're on our own and any problem we have, we solve in-house. We have almost no contact with the company with the exception of an inspection once a year. When we first started out, we had more help from the franchisor. Now we feel their attitude toward us is like it doesn't matter because we are not growing or contributing enough to warrant assistance."

From a franchisee who ran an independent studio business and then converted to Glamour Shots, a small franchise system: "The franchisor is very supportive and questions get answered very quickly. I can pick up the phone right now and speak with the president of the company, and if he's not there, I can leave a message and I know he will call me back."

CORPORATE UNITS

Size is just one of the priorities you may have. Another crucial factor for some franchisees is whether the system operates company-owned stores. The conventional wisdom is that being in the thick of daily operations makes the franchisor more aware of the franchisee's needs and can spawn ideas for improvements. In more than just a few cases, however, franchisees have been hurt by corporate stores that have situated themselves too close to the franchisee's location and, in effect, taken away from the franchisee's business.

Tip

When you first meet with the franchisor, ask what its policy is on company-owned stores. If company units are operated, find out if distance restrictions apply. What is the closest distance allowed to franchisee units? Are the distances strictly ad-hered to? Is the policy written into the franchise contract? Does the franchisor have any immediate plans to open stores in your selected area?

Besides the "cannibalism" issue, there is the oft-repeated remark that the franchisee stores are better run and more profitable than corporate stores. Although this is not the case for all franchises, in general, the sales revenues of franchisee units usually exceed those of corporate units. And for some franchisees of companies that are going through system difficulties, the reaction to company stores can be quite negative. Franchisees of two different chain restaurant systems commented: "Company-owned units should go through re-training and stop giving us franchisees a bad name," and "If someone goes into a company store that is not performing well because of lack of funds or whatever and they are not served well or don't get good food, then they are probably not going to want to go to another [another restaurant in the same chain], including mine."

PRODUCT VERSUS SERVICE FRANCHISES

When you make your priorities list, you will probably give some thought to the choice between a product and a service franchise. In essence, your choice comes down to this: Service franchises are riding a crest of popularity and are now the faster selling of the two types of franchises. However, selling services is a harder sell for the franchisee.

It is considerably harder to sell an intangible service than a tangible product. Your service can't be seen, smelled, touched or tasted. Sales efforts must concentrate on the benefits a customer receives from the service. Quite often it is difficult to evaluate the quality of a service until a service is actually performed. With a product franchise, the product itself can communicate a value to the customer, and so customers feel more secure in their buying decision, thus making it an easier sell for the franchisee.

Some of the challenges you must consider with a service franchisor:

- Your business location is more restricted to a particular location, since your market will probably be a very targeted one.

- The size of the operation is limited because the customers will purchase your time and performance rather than a mass-produced product.

- Service quality is difficult to standardize because of variations in human performance. Developing a consistency with each customer will take a special effort.

- Sales of services will depend greatly upon past customers who will give high recommendations.

As you can see from these few examples, you must consider many aspects from a variety of questions before you can come up with your priority list. Your first list of priorities will probably not be your last.

MATCHING PRIORITIES TO OPPORTUNITIES

As we interviewed franchisees, we noted that the ones who seemed to be the most satisfied and happiest in their franchise choices were those who actively set up priorities. After a period of personal analysis and investigation, these franchisees came up with maybe five or six "must-haves" for their choice. Following are the stories of four franchisees and how they managed to match their priorities with the franchise opportunity.

Finding a Franchise with Low Start-Up Costs

Arny Grushkin, based in Westport, Connecticut, was the president of a corporate subsidiary company where the economic downturn and company consolidation led to his leaving. After an unsuccessful job search, he explored independent business opportunities and then settled on franchising.

After giving it some thought, Grushkin sat down and wrote a profile of a franchise opportunity that would interest him. These were his priorities:

- ❧ No overhead.
- ❧ No salaried employees.
- ❧ Operate out of his house.
- ❧ Not selling each day (some continuity from customers).
- ❧ Residual income possibility.
- ❧ A newer franchise with prime area available for franchising.

Shortly after this, Grushkin attended one of the giant franchise shows and saw literally everything from "soup to nuts." At the very end of the show, he came upon Unishippers, a concept of economical air shipments for small and moderate business users. Unishippers fulfilled his profile requirements and a new franchisee was in business.

Entrepreneurial Qualities Influence Choice

Steve Saffar was a successful automobile agency manager who did not really enjoy his work. He made a great salary, but he also worked very long hours. He was itching for the opportunity to produce for himself and exert greater control over his life. Finally, he looked at the opportunities in both independent and franchise businesses. Choosing a franchise concept, he wrote out what he called his "guidelines" for the business. They were:

- ❧ Recession-proof business.
- ❧ Repetitive in nature.
- ❧ Not capital intensive.
- ❧ Low overhead.
- ❧ High degree of personal independence (no intensive franchisor "looking over your shoulder").

When Saffar found The Wedding Pages franchise, a wedding information publication that sells advertising, he found the right system for his guidelines.

When Regional Expansion is a Priority

When Linda Moore hit the "glass ceiling" and became annoyed with the widespread mismanagement at a *Fortune 500* corporation, she thought it was time to strike out on her own. Like most former corporate employees, she considered both independent and franchise businesses.

Rejecting an independent business for a variety of reasons, she defined her ideal franchise opportunity in terms of what she wanted and what she didn't want:

- ❧ No high-tech businesses.
- ❧ No food businesses.
- ❧ Leaning toward a professional service.
- ❧ System must be ethical and well-managed.
- ❧ Opportunity to develop a business regionally, not just operate a store or two.

Because Moore felt the regional development opportunity was an important criterion for her, her franchise system had to be relatively young with an entire region had to be available to her. A two-year old franchise called Ledger Plus, a service which does accounting, tax planning and preparation for small businesses, fit the bill. Linda Moore is now a happy regional owner for the company.

Zeroing in on a Niche Business

After Jay McDuffie decided he wasn't going to relocate with his company, he started to look at franchising. He used these guidelines in making his choice:

- ❧ Customers come to him (no making cold calls).
- ❧ A niche business, not one in a large industry with a lot of competition.
- ❧ A repeat business.
- ❧ No big loan required.

McDuffie considered several businesses—quick printing, fast-food, dry cleaning—all businesses where people would come to him and that would be repeat business. One by one, he eliminated these businesses, basically because each was too expensive to get into and each had too much competition. He eventually bought a franchise business called Check Express, a check-cashing business, which fit all his critical guidelines.

Other Considerations in Choosing a System

Several of the franchisees we talked to were not as formal in setting out their priorities, but they had a few overriding requirements that had to be met. Two of their stories follow.

Judy Gedman, a salesperson for software and hardware programs to businesses, left because of frustration with large corporations. She eventually chose a franchise in the sign industry, Fastsigns, because "it was creative, clean, computer-oriented and industry-driven." In the selection process, Judy also looked at a retail card shop and a frozen yogurt shop. She rejected these because "your location makes or breaks you. I feel it's better to go out and market something." For Judy, the Fastsigns business afforded her better control of her fate.

A Citizens Against Crime franchisee presents crime prevention seminars to businesses, Rotary Clubs and other organizations. The franchisees make money by selling safety items during and after the programs. Nancy Mann, one of the franchisees, says many choose the franchise because they have had personal experiences with a crime and have then become interested in the preventive aspects. According to Nancy, "Citizens Against Crime is a franchise where you can both feel good and make money. There are many teachers, ministers and social workers involved with the franchise." In this franchise, says Nancy, "You must care about people, not only about making money."

Poor Franchise Choices

As you might expect, every franchisee we talked to didn't, in hindsight, make the best choice possible. Unfortunately, these less-than-perfect choices generally resulted because the individual didn't rigorously analyze and investigate the various opportunities beforehand. The following franchisee story can give you an idea of how things can go wrong if the initial homework isn't done properly.

A franchisee in the retail frozen yogurt business says when he bought the first store he didn't understand what "retail" meant. Now, after opening 6 stores, he doesn't think he's really good at it. "You need to be able to size up customers, be able to predict what your customers will like or dislike, and create a certain retail atmosphere." Another problem which he did not anticipate in the business is the seasonal factor. The business falls off dramatically in the winter, and a cold winter heightens this effect. The net result is a serious cash flow problem for the franchisee during certain times of the year. If he could do it over, the franchisee would still buy a franchise, but he would look more carefully at his capabilities and the nature of the business itself.

FRANCHISING FROM HOME

The U.S. Labor Department's Bureau of Labor Statistics recently conducted a survey of home-based businesses and estimated that there are just over four million self-employed, home-based workers. (The number of franchised businesses in this total was not calculated.) However, the National Association of Home-Based Businesses, in Owings Mills, MD, puts the number at closer to 50 million people. Whatever the accurate number is, it is a number that everyone agrees will only continue to rise.

So you will undoubtedly make a choice between a home-based business or an office or storefront. Even with the growing popularity of home-based businesses, analyze this option very carefully. To be sure, the usual gut reaction today when considering working from the home is, "Great! No more commuting, no more traffic jams, no boss, no time clock." Working from homes seems to appeal to many people, but, like most of the other choices you'll make, this one requires careful thought. Working from the home is certainly not for everyone.

Some of the franchisees we interviewed had home-based businesses which ranged from business services (e.g., Leadership Management, Inc.) to cleaning services (e.g., Jani-King) and computer learning (e.g., Computertots). Their reactions to the home-based experience were mixed.

Sandi Vettle, a Leadership Management franchisee, and Fred Banty, a Padgett Business Services franchisee, both believe that an office environment is more conducive to business. Vettle began her business in her home and then switched to an office building where she found that a professional office setting improved her pro-ductivity. "Working from the home is fine only if you are a very disciplined person," says Vettle. Fred Banty also feels that an outside office is better for business, yet he remains home-based so he can be close to his three small children. Banty believes that an outside office would help with franchise name recognition and would present a more professional image. He also thinks there would be fewer distractions and business would increase if he moved out of the home.

On the other hand, Mary Cunningham, a Decorating Den franchisee, staunchly supports the home-based option. She doesn't feel that her productivity at home is lessened. "I am very disciplined and usually work seven days a week," says Cunningham. She adds that she likes "working from the home better than from an office. I still deal with people all the time, but I don't have to put up with all the personality problems in the office."

Tip

To better keep home and business activities separate, put up a plaque with the name of your business on the door to your office. When you or family members cross the threshold, it's for business reasons.

Trap

When you live and work in the same space, it's easy to feel claustrophobic. Schedule outside meetings, lunch dates, sales calls—activities that will get you away from the too-familiar setting on a regular basis.

Before making a decision on a home-based business, you will need to examine your personality, lifestyle, work habits and motives. These are some of the questions you should ask yourself:

1. *Am I self-motivated?* Without the fixed structure of a workplace, you will need a good deal of discipline and motivation to set goals and objectives on a daily and long-term basis.

2. *Do I have a reason for wanting to work out of my home other than just saving money?* If saving money is your only motive, then you're not really choosing a home-based business. Chances are the money saved won't be enough to make you happy working at home, and

it might be better to look at alternatives. Valid reasons for working at home include family obligations requiring flexible schedules, physical disabilities which inhibit movement, and a desire for a more independent lifestyle.

3. *Am I multi-talented and resourceful?* Although all franchises require many skills, a home-based one will require even more juggling of duties. You'll be the one to type the letters, send the faxes, make the sales call and handle the filing.

4. *Am I comfortable working alone?* If you need to have people around you all the time to be happy and effective, the home-based option isn't for you. You should feel confident working on your own.

5. *Does your house have the necessary space and facilities for operating a business?* You must have a permanent work area with sufficient space and equipment. In addition to office furniture, you may also need a computer, fax machine, printer and answering machine. You might also need storage space, as well as additional electrical circuits and extra lines.

6. *Will your family support your decision to operate a home-based franchise?* With your family space overlapping business space, the entire family must understand that some areas will be out of bounds and that the privacy of the business area must be respected.

If you become part of the trend of operating a new, small business from your home, you will have an increasing variety of businesses to choose from. Businesses that can be started from a home location include financial services, residential and commercial cleaning services, direct mail, computer classes and publishing businesses.

Trap

The biggest problem with working from home is not that you won't work enough, but that you will overwork! You'll be constantly reminded of projects to be completed and phone calls that need to be returned. It's possible to work all hours of the day, all week long. Resist the temptation and put up a "Business Is Closed" sign at the appropriate times.

Tip

If you opt for a home-based franchise, check with your accountant. A 1998 change in federal tax law allows more people to deduct the cost of maintaining a home office from their income.

SELECTING YOUR WORK HOURS

Remember in Chapter 2, where I said that the ability to work hard is a given for readers of this book? Well, it's still a given, but if the number of hours worked is a priority for you, a non-negotiable item, you should consider some things carefully.

In general, new franchisees say they work harder and longer hours than they ever did in their previous jobs. Most also say they work considerably longer hours than they expected, 80 hours a week in some cases. And, although many franchisees said the long hours left them feeling tired and worn-out, they also felt the long hours were necessary to build their businesses.

However, we find the time commitments differ, depending upon the type of business. So when making your initial choice, you should investigate this aspect carefully. In general, you'll find the following is true for 3 of the main types of franchises:

Business Service Franchises

Most often you run the business the way you expect it to be run. The franchisor generally will not require adherence to a specific schedule. You will set the specific hours and days you work. This sort of franchise does give you a great deal of latitude and independence in terms of time management.

Retail Business Franchises

As a business operator in a mall or strip center, you will be required to follow its regulations. This usually implies long hours, maybe from nine or ten in the morning to eight or nine at night, and generally there is a six- or seven-day workweek. There is little or no room for deviation in operating hours, so you are locked into a rigid schedule. You are given somewhat more latitude if your retail business is in a free-standing structure. You won't have mall developers or strip center operators to answer to.

Child-Care Franchises

This business normally coincides with school hours and parent's working hours. Child-care hours generally run from 6:30 a.m. to 6:30 p.m., Monday through Friday, and the centers can only close for a few national holidays. The trend seems to be toward adding extra hours for "night care" and "sick care," so it appears that hours may be getting even longer.

When comparing the hours you would like to work with the requirements of a particular franchise business, there is one mitigating circumstance. Although some businesses have long hours and long work weeks "built-in," the demands on the franchise owner may be temporary. Many franchise owners tell of excruciatingly long hours for the first few years of the business. But once the business prospers and more employees are brought in, the work schedule becomes more reasonable.

FRANCHISE OPPORTUNITIES TO TAKE YOU INTO THE 21ST CENTURY

Unless you've decided to invest in a large, superstar franchise with a ready-made market, you'll probably explore various businesses, looking for the ones in the "hottest" areas, the ones deemed most likely to succeed. The problem is that everyone doesn't necessarily agree on the best business to make more money more quickly. You'll have to be the ultimate judge on that.

Certain types of franchising have had success in different eras. For example, in the 1950s, the building of the interstate highway system was a boon for the fast-food franchises. McDonald's, Kentucky Fried Chicken, Elias Big Boy and other restaurants were excellent investments. Today's marketplace favors some different areas.

These franchise areas should experience good growth into the 21st century. The five selections that follow capitalize on demographic, social, economic and psychodynamic trends (in the U.S.).

Business Services

Corporate downsizing has been a boon to business service franchises, and the trend is very likely to continue even though businesses have been downsizing less in the last few years. They have, however, become used to operating with a leaner staff and the resulting increased bottom line. Hundreds of services once performed in-house are now being purchased from outside businesses.

Look for franchises with functions such as consulting, accounting, training programs, product design, corporate travel, legal services, data processing, computer maintenance, website development, voice messaging, advertising and temporary help. Some print shop franchises are offering computer, tele-conferencing, video conferencing and meeting rooms to capitalize on this trend.

Tip

Think about this. A business service franchise could work very well with a team of owners—almost like a corporate business setting. It's a way to spread the operating responsibilities and the financial obligations and recreate a familiar setting for doing business.

Child-Related Businesses

It is estimated that about 30 million children under the age of 13 live in single-parent households where the parent is working or in households where both parents work. A good deal of the growth in child-related franchises can be attributed to this statistic. Look for franchises such as exercise gyms, pre-school sports and health programs, nanny services, day-care centers, teaching programs and computer training to take advantage of this trend.

Products and Services for the Older American

At the other end of the demographic spectrum, we have a growing aging population. The baby boomers will all turn 50 by the year 2005. Their life expectancy climbs a little each year and these former "flower children" want to live forever. Look for franchises dealing with health care, such as in-home health care, medical products and personnel agencies for health care workers. Travel and leisure activities for the older population are also good segments, as well as computer training franchises. Courses that teach students how to use the Internet are especially popular with older people. Franchises that sell nutritional and beauty products are also good bets.

Food Services that Deliver Quality and Variety

In the mature marketplace of food service and restaurants, one area holds great promise for explosive growth. Given today's frantic pace and stressful lifestyles, the increase in the number of two-income families and a general trend toward take-out food, which is fresh, varied and of a high quality, the food segment called "home-meal replacement" (HMR) should be a winner. Most of the large established food systems don't serve food that fits this criteria and, certainly, the once top contender in this segment, Boston Market, has failed badly with a recent bankruptcy filing. Look for newer, smaller food franchises that are creating menus and systems specifically to cater to this discerning, time-challenged segment of the population.

Everyday Services

Today's population has a larger disposable income, but less time to spend it. All of the general service companies that focus on the consumer can benefit from this. Look for services such as cleaning, lawn care, decorating, car repairs while you work, laundry pick-up at work and other time-saving services. In general, necessary products and services that can be delivered to the consumer in a fast and efficient manner will excel.

So, if you're beginning to explore franchise opportunities, the five above areas are a good place to start. Once you choose your area, then zero in on specific name franchises.

Final Words

Examine your needs, desires and capabilities before you start to talk to franchisors. Write down your "non-negotiable" constraints and then begin to look at systems which fit your requirements.

4

How Can I Be Sure I Won't Lose Money?

*Be patient. Don't settle for anything less
than the right franchise in the right
location.*
>   HAROLD SANCHEZ
>   General Nutrition Center franchisee

*No matter how much training and help the
system gives you, the success is created
by the owner.*
>   STUART RUBEN
>   Money Mailer franchisee

How can you be sure you won't lose money? You can never be sure you won't lose money, but you can greatly improve your chances of making money.

Draw up a list of your priorities and then start to investigate those franchises that best fit these priorities. Attending one of the giant franchise shows is an easy way to acquaint yourself with the realm of possibilities. But, unless you're an old hand at these events, it's easy to leave with nothing more than a shopping bag of promotional gadgets and a confusing jumble of information. It helps if you arrive at the show armed with some basic knowledge.

At many franchise and business opportunities shows, some of the exhibitors are not actually franchises. Many of the exhibitors will offer "business opportunities" and "multi-level marketing plans." If you have decided to confine your choice to franchising, don't be side-tracked by other business modes.

Here are a couple of tips to help you make the most of your expo outing.

Tracking down the franchises is not always an easy task. You probably won't know the type of organization just by the name, the product or the service. You must ask a representative of the company to explain how it does business to find out if you are dealing with a franchise system.

What's the big difference between franchises and other business modes? If the company is offering franchises it must issue a Uniform Franchise Offering Circular (UFOC) that conforms to Federal Trade Commissions (FTC) regulations. The UFOC will provide the prospective franchisee with a great deal of important information.

So rule #1 is to make sure that you're dealing with a bona fide franchise.

Rule #2 is simple. Don't just walk around. Do look carefully at the directory and decide on the companies that you wish to meet, make a list of questions and systematically go meet representatives from those companies.

Once this initial contacting is done, you're free to browse and window shop to find new and unexpected opportunities.

STARTING THE INVESTIGATION

Contact the franchise systems you are interested in—either by talking to company representatives at one of the shows or by consulting a directory that lists the different franchise opportunities in all the different business sectors.

One of the best directories on the market is *Bond's Franchise Guide*, a 500-page annual guide that covers over 2,200 franchises and includes roughly 1,100 very detailed profiles of major franchise systems. See the last page for more information on this publication. In any case, you should contact the franchise development department in the systems that appear to fit your priorities. In most cases, you will receive an information package from the company. It will probably contain a letter, a brochure describing the business and a qualifying questionnaire.

The next step is for the franchisor to send you the "Uniform Franchise Offering Circular" (UFOC) for the particular business. The UFOC was a response to exploitation by unethical individuals and con artists in the 1960s and 1970s. Today franchises are regulated by law. The Federal Trade Commission (FTC) requires that certain information be disclosed to potential franchisees before a contract can be signed or any payment made. The information is presented to the prospective franchisee in the form of a document—the UFOC.

The FTC requires franchisors in every state to provide a UFOC. In addition, some states require that the offering must first be approved and registered by the state before it can be promoted to prospective franchise buyers. These states include: California, Hawaii, Illinois, Indiana, Maryland, Michigan, Minnesota, New York, North Dakota, Oregon, Rhode Island, South Dakota, Virginia, Washington and Wisconsin. Certain states, such as Illinois and Minnesota, have even more stringent requirements for the franchisor. This in turn affords better protection for the prospective franchisee.

The UFOC contains 23 items of information that must be current as of the completion of the franchisor's most recent fiscal year. If there is a material change to the information in the document, the franchisor must make a revision (to be issued quarterly). The disclosure document must be given to a prospective franchisee at whichever occurs earlier: the first personal meeting of franchisor and prospective franchisee or ten working days prior to the execution of a contract or money payment to the franchisor.

Tip

Although the FTC requires that specific information be given to the prospective franchisee, note that the FTC does not check the contained information and will not vouch for its accuracy. Nothing will take the place of your own investigative activities.

The 23 items of information in a UFOC are as follows:

1. *The franchisor and any predecessor.* This section contains historical background material on the franchisor, as well as any predecessors. It includes corporate and trade names, address and principal place of business. A description of the franchise should include information such as the nature of the franchise and business experience of the franchisor, including direct experience in a franchise.

2. *Identity and business experience of persons affiliated with the franchisor.* All names of individuals having significant responsibilities in the operation of the business or in support services provided to the franchisees must be disclosed. Information stating the person's current position in the company and business experience for the last five years is also included. If a marketing representative or franchise broker is involved, the same information is required.

3. *Litigation history.* Detailed information on criminal, civil and administrative litigation involving any of the officers, owners, directors or key executives of the company is disclosed in this section if the allegations or proceedings would concern the potential franchisee.

4. *Bankruptcy history.* The franchisor must disclose whether the company or any of its directors or officers has filed for bankruptcy during the past 15 years. Information on each action must be included.

5. *Franchisee's initial franchise fee and/or other initial payment.* This section states the franchise fee and any other initial payments to be made by the franchisee upon the execution of the franchise agreement. The section discloses the terms of payment and fees, the use of such monies, and whether the payment and fees are refundable in whole or in part.

6. *Other fees.* All other fees are detailed, including royalties, advertising fees, insurance expenses, training costs, audit and accounting cost, consulting, leases, alteration costs and any other fees associated with the franchise.

7. *Franchisee's estimated initial investment.* The estimated expenditures associated with the opening of a franchise are recounted with a high and low range given for real estate, construction, equipment, fixtures, permits, furnishings, signage, inventory, working capital, etc. This section should include the name of the person or persons to whom payment is made for the preceding, under what terms and whether refund terms apply.

8. *Obligations of franchisee to purchase or lease from designated sources.* Any requirements that the franchisee must purchase goods, services, supplies, equipment or insurance for the opening and/or operation of the franchise from a franchisor-designated source must be disclosed. Franchisors must also disclose if they receive income from the approved suppliers as a result of purchases by franchisees.

9. *Obligations of franchisee to purchase or lease in accordance with specifications or from approved suppliers.* A further elaboration on supply sourc-

ing, this section itemizes any responsibility of the franchisee to purchase or lease either from pre-approved suppliers or according to franchisor specifications. Specifications for purchases are not normally included, but pricing, discounts and procedures to have suppliers approved by the franchisor are usually cited.

Tip

Two important questions that should be answered by the franchisor are: Is the franchisee obligated to buy any (or all) supplies from the franchisor? If not, do franchisee-chosen suppliers have to be approved?

10. *Financing arrangements.* Any financing programs that are offered either by the franchisor or its designates are described in this section.

11. *Obligations of franchisor: other supervision, assistance or services.* This section describes the initial and on-going services and support of the franchisor. Often it is divided into two parts—service obligations of the franchisor and services that may be performed by the franchisor. Some types of service and support described are training, advertising material, site selection, market research and computer services.

12. *Territorial rights.* If the franchisor grants exclusive rights, the territory and the rights will be described in this section. Any conditions that the franchisee must meet to retain these rights, as well as the rights of the franchisor, are also disclosed.

13. *Trademarks, service marks, trade names, logo types and commercial symbols.* The franchisor must disclose information regarding the registration of trademarks, service marks, trade names, logo types and commercial symbols with the U.S. Patent and Trademark Office. Also included is a list of states and countries in which the marks

are registered, as well as any limitations imposed on the franchisee for the use of these marks.

14. *Patents and copyrights.* This disclosure lists any patents and copyrights that may be involved in the operation of the franchise and that may cover trade secrets and confidential information.

15. *Obligation of the franchisee to participate in the operation of the franchise business.* If the franchisor requires the active participation of the franchisee in the operation of the business, it must be so stated. Terms and conditions of the participation should be defined.

16. *Restrictions on goods and services offered by franchisee.* Any limits or exclusions on goods and services that can be commercialized by the franchisee are stated in this section.

17. *Renewal, termination, repurchase, modification and assignment of the franchise agreement and related information.* This, the longest and most complex section, covers the franchisor's requirements and the franchisee's options when a franchise is to be renewed, terminated, repurchased, modified or assigned.

18. *Arrangements with public figures.* If the franchisor has any compensation or endorsement program with a public figure, it must be disclosed. If the public figure is involved in the ownership or the management of the franchise, it must also be disclosed.

Trap

Don't get fooled into thinking a franchise is better than it is just because a celebrity is associated with it. Base your decision on your investigative analysis of the franchise.

19. *Actual, average, projected or forecasted franchise sales, profits or earnings.* There is an option here. Some franchisors will state that they do not furnish the actual, average, projected or forecasted sales and

earnings to prospective franchisees. If a franchisor does make a claim of sales, profits or earnings, then the franchisor must fully describe the method by which the claim is made.

20. *Information regarding franchises of the franchisor.* The franchisor provides a summary of franchises sold, the number actually operating, the number of agreements signed but not in operation, and the number of company-owned units. Information on the number of franchises terminated or not renewed with the causes for termination or non-renewal for the past three years is also required.

21. *Financial statements.* In this section there is a complete set of financial statements, usually a balance sheet for the past fiscal year, an income statement and changes in the financial position of the franchisor for the most recent three fiscal years. Most states require audited statements.

Tip

The financial statements of new franchise systems will probably not be very impressive, since they have had no opportunity to establish a track record. In this case, concentrate more on evaluating the business concept and the management.

22. *Franchise agreement and related documents.* A copy of the franchise document and any other document to be signed by the franchisee must be included as exhibits.

23. *Acknowledgment of receipt by a prospective franchise.* Prospective franchisees are required to sign an acknowledgment that a disclosure document was received from the franchisor.

Trap

Don't fall for the franchisor who treats the UFOC as a company secret and requires that you visit the corporate headquarters prior to seeing their UFOC. The UFOC should be carefully analyzed before contemplating a visit to corporate headquarters.

Tip

One of the best ways to be sure you won't lose money is to work in the franchise before buying. Some prospective franchisees even work in the franchise for no money—just to be sure there are no big surprises when they sign the contract!

LOCATION, LOCATION, LOCATION

Here's one important bit of information you must never forget. *A poorly selected site for a franchise will most likely mean failure—even if the concept is great!* Since this chapter is about ways to ensure you don't lose money, I would be remiss if I did not stress the prime importance of a superior location.

The location of a fast-food business can make or break it. Camille and Edward DiNapoli, Subway franchisees, feel that location is by far the most important aspect of the business. Before opening, Camille and her husband spent a lot of time looking at neighborhood demographics, traffic patterns and parking facilities. One neighboring franchisee is struggling because there is almost no parking available for the shop, although all other factors are acceptable.

Be very careful before signing up for a business located in a mall or strip center. You need only listen to those who have tried it and report that the mall or strip developers are a bigger factor than the franchise system in regulating hours and imposing regulations and restrictions. As some have only half-jokingly said, "Landlords take the second syllable in their name far too seriously."

A mall developer's influence on your business is great but you have even less control over the management of the mall. With an incompetent management, the quality of the mall can be destroyed. Then, too, in many instances the developers are almost like your financial partners because of lease arrangements that stipulate an additional payment to the landlord when the franchisee goes over an agreed-upon sales figure. In those cases, the landlord has the right to audit sales figures. So, consider such locations carefully before signing the lease.

Tip

Don't overlook the obvious when picking a location. Customers are not going to ride around and around looking for a parking space so they can use your products or services.

However, for some types of franchises, location is less important. Let's say you want to open a tax and accounting service. You still need to conduct marketing and demographic assessments to situate yourself in an area where there is a market demand. But since you will often be traveling to the customer's place of business, and since you don't rely on foot traffic, the convenience of your location isn't as critical.

Tip

College campuses can be great locations for service businesses. Poll students first to determine which services they need and want on campus. This almost ensures success!

Don't be so eager to open your franchise that you don't spend enough time looking at and assessing locations. Harold Sanchez, a GNC (General Nutrition Center, a retail health products store) franchisee, made that mistake. He says, "I got nudgy to get into business after taking a separation package from my corporation and took a location that the franchisor had settled on even though I had grave misgivings about it." Now Sanchez realizes that his business will not reach its full potential at the present location, and he is contemplating the expense and trouble of moving it elsewhere.

The best type of structure for your business will also be a determinant of the location. Sometimes personal preference is the decisive factor here. For example, Jeff Grayson has a different setup with each of his Pizzeria Uno restaurants. One restaurant is in an indoor mall, one is in a strip center and one is free-standing. Grayson likes the free-standing location best of all. He says, "It's individualistic and you're not hit with the percentage rates [on rents] that you have in malls and centers." (For help in choosing a location, fill out the site selection worksheet in Figure 4.5 at the end of the chapter.)

Tip

Think about opening your franchise on a military base if your products and services are appropriate. This ready-made market proved just right for a KFC franchise on a U.S. Army base in Fort Campbell, Kentucky, and a Domino's Pizza franchise on a U.S. Marine base in California.

QUIZZING CURRENT FRANCHISEES

After you have read and analyzed a franchisor's offering document (the UFOC), and if you are still interested in pursuing the opportunity then it's time to start telephoning. You'll be calling or visiting franchisees and plying them with questions. *This is a step you can't skip!*

Turn to the exhibit section of the UFOC, where most franchisors include a list of current franchisees, their complete names, addresses and telephone numbers. If this information is not included, the franchisor should furnish it to you upon your request. In addition, most franchisors list franchisees "who have been terminated, canceled, not renewed or have voluntarily or involuntarily ceased to operate the business during the current year."

It's difficult to give an *absolute* number of franchisees who should be called. The size of the system has a lot to do with it. If there are only five franchisees, you should call all five. But in the larger systems, you'll have to use

81

your judgment. Try to get a good cross-section of franchisees, and don't forget to call several of the franchisees who voluntarily or involuntarily left the system.

What will you talk to them about? You will ask them about all the things that are important to you. Glenn and Connie Schenenga, Future Kids (computer training) franchisees, spoke to many of the 40 or 50 franchisees listed and asked them questions like, "Are you making any money? Are you happy? What are the positives and negatives of the business?" Pretty basic questions, but ones that every prospective franchisee would like to know the answers to. You might also inquire about the hours involved in running the business, the relationship of franchisee and franchisor and, of course, when the franchisees turned their first profit.

If you contact a wide cross-section, you will undoubtedly encounter struggling, surviving, successful and super-successful franchisees. Try to determine, as best you can, why some are not succeeding. Is the franchisee taking advantage of the corporate support? Is the franchisee putting in the time? Perhaps the owner is an absentee one. Is the franchisee out selling? The point is to try and find out if the problems lie with the franchisee or with the franchise system.

CALCULATING POTENTIAL SALES, CASH FLOW AND PROFIT

Calculating the potential sales, cash flow and profit of a franchise business is a key element in choosing a profit-making franchise. This job is not always as easy as it should be. Neither the Federal Trade Commission (FTC) nor any of the states require a franchisor to tell how well franchisees have done in the past or estimate how much a new franchisee is likely to earn. However, franchisors are allowed to provide a voluntary written "earnings claim" in their offering circular. About 32% of franchisors currently choose to make this voluntary statement. The good news is that competitive pressures will certainly continue to increase the number of franchisors that include earnings claims. An appropriate starting point might be to consult the book *"How Much Can I Make?"* by Robert Bond. This book includes over 145 recent earnings claim statements for franchises in 46 different industry categories. So even though you may not find your specific franchise earnings information, you can check out earnings of other franchise systems in the same industry.

Your chosen franchise business should supply you with some figures of average sales in the franchisee units. Figure 4.1 is examples of how franchisors present this information in their offering circulars.

Figure 4.1 Sample Franchising Earnings Claims

Burger King Corporation, franchisor of Burger King fast-food restaurants, supplies Average Unit Sales estimates in Item 19 of the 1996 UFOC. Restaurants used in calculation of Average Sales consisted of 5,901 "traditional" and 495 "nontraditional." Nontraditional sites include: (1) "expressway" facilities serving a limited menu; (2) restaurants at institutional locations (such as airports, colleges, hospitals, tourist locations, etc.); (3) co-branded facilities and (4) restaurants at double drive-thru facilities.

Median Sales for franchised traditional restaurants is $1,081,970 and $716,341 for nontraditional restaurants.

Traditional Restaurants	**Company**	**Franchise**
Low Annual Sales	$309,073	$203,478
High Annual Sales	$2,368,460	$2,640,276
Median Sales	$1,109,095	$1,081,970

Nontraditional Restaurants	**Company**	**Franchise**
Low Annual Sales	$302,545	$66,740
High Annual Sales	$2,199,993	$3,796,189
Median Sales	$547,311	$716,341

Item 19 of the Uniform Franchise Offering Circular of December 31, 1996.
Burger King Corporation, 1777 Old Cutler Rd., Miami, FL 33157.

Holiday Hospitality Franchising, franchisor of the Holiday Inn Hotels, offers information on the Average Room Rate, Average Occupancy Rate and Average Revenue Per Available Room in Item 19 of the UFOC. The following information is for the fiscal year October, 1996 to September, 1997. The averages that follow represent information for all 1,884 franchised Holiday Inn hotels in operation, including 20 Holiday Inn Sunspree Resort Hotels, 4 Crowne Plaza Resort Hotels, 1,092 Holiday Inn Hotels, 584 Holiday Inn Express Hotels, 67 Holiday Inn Select's, 28 Holiday Inn Hotels & Suites and 41 Holiday Inn Express Hotel & Suites.

Average Room Rate	$68.18
Average Occupancy Rate	65.6%
Average Revenue Per Available Room (RPAR)	$44.74

Average Room Rate was calculated by dividing total amount of room rental revenues by total number of guest rooms rented. A total of 584 hotels, or 31%, in the study achieved or surpassed this average room rate.

Average Occupancy Rate was calculated by dividing the number of guest room nights reported rented by total number of rooms available for rent. A total of 868 hotels, or 46.1%, in the study achieved or surpassed this rate.

The RPAR was calculated by multiplying the Average Room Rate for each hotel by its Average Occupancy Rate. A total of 661 hotels, or 35.1%, in the study achieved or surpassed this RPAR.

Item 19 of the Uniform Franchise Offering Circular of January, 1998.

Holiday Hospitality Franchising, Three Ravina Dr., Atlanta, GA 30346.

In Item 19 of its UFOC, Jiffy Lube International, Inc., franchisor of Jiffy Lube "quick lube" service centers, discloses earnings claims. There were 413 stations that were in operation for the full 12 months of 1996—all were company-owned. The following table divides the 413 stations into three groups on the basis of median gross sales level.

Number of Centers	Range of Gross Sales	Median Gross Sales
138 Centers	$181,032–$417,490	$350,374
138 Centers	$417,555–$566,127	$475,283
137 Centers	$567,120–$1,337,743	$738,931

Item 19 of the Uniform Franchise Offering Circular of March 31, 1997.

Jiffy Lube International, Inc., 700 Milam St., Houston, TX 77002.

Calculating Average Gross Sales

Many franchisors have withheld earnings claim statements because they fear lawsuits in the event that the projections fall short. Unfortunately, this means prospective franchise investors have to take a roundabout way to come up with the appropriate numbers.

One way to calculate average gross sales per franchise when no earnings claim is available is the following:

1. Check the franchisor's audited financials for the total royalty payments to them from franchisees.

2. In the offering document, find the percentage of gross sales the franchisees pay out as royalties (the royalty rate).

3. Calculate the number of full-time operating franchises. Exclude the company-owned stores from this total.

4. Divide the total royalty payments by the number of franchisees. This is the average royalty payment per franchisee.

5. Then divide this number by the royalty rate to calculate the average gross sales per franchisee.

Let's take a simple example to show you how this works. The franchisor shows $2 million in royalty payments from franchisees in its financial statements. The system has 100 operating franchises and two company-owned stores. So we will divide $2 million (total royalties) by 100 and we find that $20,000 is the average royalty payment. The royalty rate is 5%. We then divide 20,000 by 0.05 (5%) and find that $400,000 is the average gross sale per franchise. (Refer to Figure 4.2 to help you with your calculations.)

Figure 4.2 Worksheet for Average Gross Sales per Franchisee

1. Total Royalty Amount franchisor receives from franchisees: $_____

2. Royalty Rate   _____%

3. Number of Operating Franchised Units
(no company-owned units)   _____

4. Average Royalty Payment per franchisee
*(Total Royalty Amount [#1] divided by Number
of Franchised Units [#3])* $_____

5. Average Gross Sales per franchisee
*(Average Royalty Payment per franchisee divided by
the Royalty Rate [#2])* $_____

Projecting Cash Flow

Cash flow is the difference between what your business takes in and what you spend. The technique used to anticipate cash needs is called a "cash flow analysis." The cash flow analysis will tell you when you are likely to have either a cash shortage, or a cash surplus. Your purpose in putting together these cash flow numbers is to get a picture of whether your working capital is sufficient to operate the business.

Let's say your initial investment for XYZ franchise is $50,000, including the franchise fee and start-up equipment, furniture and rent. You have $70,000 ($40,000 from a home equity loan, and $30,000 from your savings). This leaves you with $20,000 for operating or working capital. What you will then want to determine is: Will the $20,000 be enough to get the business through the startup phase or will there be a shortfall, necessitating a scramble for more funds?

Where do you start? You start looking at the projected annual sales. (That's why it's very important that the franchisor supply you with this very basic historical information). Let's say projected annual sales in your state (or region) for the chosen franchise is $250,000. To project your cash flow needs, you can simply divide this figure by 12 and you will have an estimated monthly sales figure. If, however, by talking to present franchisees, you know that there is a seasonal skew—sales are not evenly balanced throughout the year—you should work this into your sales projections.

Interestingly enough, some major fast-food franchisees we interviewed said there was even a seasonality in their business. They had heavier sales in the spring and summer seasons. Of course, if you're in the business of preparing taxes, you can project your busiest period to be the first third of the year. So, if you detect a seasonality to the proposed business, build this into your projections by showing greater than one-twelfth of the sales total at some times of the year and less in other months.

	Jan.	Feb.	Mar.	Apr.	May
1. Beginning Cash	30,000	5,734	7,031	8,328	10,125
Plus:					
2. Cash Sales	14,000	14,000	14,000	13,000	13,000
3. Credit Sales	0	7,500	7,500	7,500	6,500
4. Bank Loan	40,000				
5. Total Cash Available	84,000	27,234	28,531	28,828	29,625
Less:					
6. Purchases	16,125	8,063	8,063	6,563	7,313
7. Wages, Including Taxes	4,821	4,821	4,821	4,821	4,821
8. Supplies	75	75	75	75	75
9. Advertising	150	150	150	150	150
10. Rent	2,400	2,400	2,400	2,400	2,400
11. Real Estate Taxes	75	75	75	75	75
12. Telephone, Electricity	520	520	520	520	520
13. Insurance	350	350	350	350	350
14. Interest	267	267	267	267	267
15. Royalty	430	430	430	390	390
16. Miscellaneous	1,320	2,320	2,320	2,360	2,360
17. Franchise Fee	25,000	0	0	0	0
18. Start-up Equipment	25,000	0	0	0	0
19. Total Cash Expenditure	76,533	19,470	19,470	17,970	18,720
20. Net Cash Available	7,467	7,764	9,061	10,858	10,905
Less:					
21. Distribution To Owner	500	500	500	500	500
22. Loan Fee	1,000				
23. Loan Amortization	233	233	233	233	233
24. Ending Cash Balance	5,734	7,031	8,328	10,125	10,172
Loan Balance	39,767	39,534	39,301	39,068	38,835

Figure 4.3 Cash Flow Statement
Best Franchise Inc. (Dan Lasman, Hampstead Partners Inc., Wilton, CT).

June	July	Aug.	Sept.	Oct.	Nov.	Dec.	Year 1 Total	Year 2 Total
10,172	10,218	11,140	9,625	8,109	5,218	6,265	30,000	7,312
13,000	12,000	12,000	12,000	14,000	16,000	18,000	165,000	181,500
6,500	6,500	5,000	5,000	5,000	7,500	8,500	73,000	92,528
							40,000	
29,672	28,718	28,140	26,625	27,109	28,718	32,765	308,000	281,340
7,313	5,438	6,375	6,375	9,750	10,313	13,313	105,000	115,500
4,821	4,821	4,821	4,821	4,821	4,821	4,821	57,852	57,852
75	75	75	75	75	75	75	900	900
150	150	150	150	150	150	150	1,800	1,800
2,400	2,400	2,400	2,400	2,400	2,400	2,400	28,800	28,800
75	75	75	75	75	75	75	900	900
520	520	520	520	520	520	520	6,240	6,240
350	350	350	350	350	350	350	4,200	4,200
267	267	267	267	267	267	267	3,200	3,200
390	340	340	340	430	490	600	5,000	
2,360	2,410	2,410	2,410	2,320	2,260	2,150	27,000	33,000
0	0	0	0	0	0	0	25,000	
0	0	0	0	0	0	0	25,000	
18,720	16,845	17,783	17,783	21,158	21,720	24,720	290,892	252,392
10,951	11,873	10,358	8,842	5,951	6,998	8,045	17,108	28,948
500	500	500	500	500	500	500	6,000	12,000
							1,000	
233	233	233	233	233	233	233	2,796	2,796
10,218	11,140	9,625	8,109	5,218	6,265	7,312	7,312	14,152
38,602	38,369	38,136	37,903	37,670	37,437	37,204	37,204	34,408

After you have estimated sales for each month of the year, you will need this additional information:

1. If you're buying a cash business, you already have your cash receipts each month from your estimated sales figures. If, however, you will be extending credit to customers, there will be a time lapse between the time of the sale and the time that the funds are deposited into your bank account.

Trap

The time lag between making the sale and collecting the money is the reason most businesses get into cash flow problems. You will have to pay your suppliers for goods and services even if you're not paid on time. If your business is known for slow-paying customers (find out from other franchisees), you may need double the working capital you anticipated.

2. If your business extends credit, then you must put the credit terms into your projections. For example, if your credit terms are net invoice payable in 30 days, you will show a sale in January, for example, but the receivable will be noted as paid in February. If you want to see more of the downside, show payment in March, allowing for late payments.

3. Then you must make a list of expenditures (cash outlays) for the month. This includes: cost of goods/purchases (get these figures from the franchisor), rent, loan payments, payroll, supplies, advertising, telephone, utilities, insurance, royalties to franchisor and other miscellaneous payments. You may want to split the expenditures into two types: fixed monthly payments such as rent, and variable payments, such as royalties.

4. Now you simply add up the incoming cash and collections for total cash available. Then add up all the monthly expenditures for total cash paid out. Finally, subtract the total cash paid out from

the total cash available, and you will have your cash position or net cash available. (If you do not intend to take a monthly cash distribution at first and if you have no debt to service, stop right here.)

5. From the net cash available, you will then subtract your salary (distribution to owner). Then subtract the debt service amount (loan amortization) for the ending cash balance.

When you're all finished with your calculations, analyze the results. If the cash position comes up negative several times and you can't increase your working capital, you might need to rethink your choice of franchise investment. (See Figure 4.3 for a sample cash flow setup.)

Tip

If you are completely unfamiliar with cash flow projections or don't feel confident enough to put together a projection, do it with your accountant. In any case, don't skip this very important part of your franchise analysis.

Profit and Loss Statement

Lastly, you'll put together a projected profit and loss (P&L) statement for a two-year period. The good news is that most of the numbers are already there if you have already calculated annual sales and made the cash flow projections.

For your P&L statement, do the following:

1. Take your anticipated first-year sales and subtract from that the cost of the sales or the cost of the goods sold. Cost of goods sold is equal to the beginning inventory plus the purchases less the ending inventory. This gives you your gross margin number.

	Jan.	Feb.	Mar.	Apr.	May
1. Cash Sales	14,000	14,000	14,000	13,000	13,000
2. Credit Sales	7,500	7,500	7,500	6,500	6,500
3. Total Sales	21,500	21,500	21,500	19,500	19,500
Cost of Goods Sold:					
4. Beginning Inventory	0	8,063	8,063	8,063	7,313
5. Purchases	16,125	8,063	8,063	6,563	7,313
6. Goods Available	16,125	16,125	16,125	14,625	14,625
7. (Less Ending Inventory)	(8,063)	(8,063)	(8,063)	(7,313)	(7,313)
8. Cost of Goods Sold	8,062	8,062	8,062	7,312	7,313
9. Gross Margin	13,438	13,438	13,438	12,188	12,188
Operating Expenses:					
10. Wages, Including Taxes	4,821	4,821	4,821	4,821	4,821
11. Supplies	75	75	75	75	75
12. Advertising	150	150	150	150	150
13. Rent	2,400	2,400	2,400	2,400	2,400
14. Real Estate Taxes	75	75	75	75	75
15. Telephone, Electricity	520	520	520	520	520
16. Insurance	350	350	350	350	350
17. Royalty	430	430	430	390	390
18. Miscellaneous	2,320	2,320	2,320	2,360	2,360
19. Depreciation & Amortization	833	833	833	833	833
20. Total Operating Expenses	11,974	11,974	11,974	11,974	11,974
21. Operating Income	1,464	1,464	1,464	214	214
22. Interest	267	267	267	267	267
23. Net Income/(Loss)	1,197	1,197	1,197	(54)	(54)

Figure 4.4 Profit and Loss Statement
Best Franchise Inc. (Dan Lasman, Hampstead Partners Inc., Wilton, CT).

June	July	Aug.	Sept.	Oct.	Nov.	Dec.	Year 1 Total	Year 2 Total
13,000	12,000	12,000	12,000	14,000	16,000	18,000	165,000	181,500
6,500	5,000	5,000	5,000	7,500	8,500	12,000	85,000	93,500
19,500	17,000	17,000	17,000	21,500	24,500	30,000	250,000	275,000
7,313	7,313	6,375	6,375	6,375	8,063	9,188	0	11,250
7,313	5,438	6,375	6,375	9,750	10,313	13,313	105,000	115,500
14,625	12,750	12,750	12,750	16,125	18,375	22,500	105,000	126,750
(7,313)	(6,375)	(6,375)	(6,375)	(8,063)	(9,188)	(11,250)	(11,250)	(12,375)
7,313	6,375	6,375	6,375	8,062	9,187	11,250	93,750	114,375
12,188	10,625	10,625	10,625	13,438	15,313	18,750	156,250	160,625
4,821	4,821	4,821	4,821	4,821	4,821	4,821	57,852	57,852
75	75	75	75	75	75	75	900	900
150	150	150	150	150	150	150	1,800	1,800
2,400	2,400	2,400	2,400	2,400	2,400	2,400	28,800	28,800
75	75	75	75	75	75	75	900	900
520	520	520	520	520	520	520	6,240	6,240
350	350	350	350	350	350	350	4,200	4,200
390	340	340	340	430	490	600	5,000	5,000
2,360	2,410	2,410	2,140	2,320	2,260	2,150	28,000	28,000
833	833	833	833	833	833	833	9,996	9,996
11,974	11,974	11,974	11,974	11,974	11,974	11,974	143,688	143,688
214	(1,349)	(1,349)	(1,349)	1,464	3,339	6,776	12,562	16,937
267	267	267	267	267	267	267	3,204	2,976
(54)	(1,616)	(1,616)	(1,616)	1,197	3,072	6,509	9,358	13,961

2. Next, add up all your expenditures for the year from your cash flow statement; this number will be your total expenses. Be sure to add accrued expenses plus non-cash expenses such as depreciation. To better understand this part of the P&L statement, two definitions are necessary: Depreciation and amortization are sister concepts, with the distinction that depreciation deals with tangible assets and amortization with intangible assets. The concept of allocating the cost of a tangible asset over its useful life is depreciation. For example, if a company buys a machine for $1 million and the machinery has a useful life of five years, the machinery is depreciated or "expensed" over a period of five years at a rate of $200,000 per year. Amortization refers to the allocation of the cost of an intangible asset over its useful life. For example, if an individual buys a franchise and pays a franchise fee of $20,000, the franchise fee would probably be amortized over five years at a rate of $4,000 per year. (In the case of our example, Figure 4.4, the start-up equipment cost of $25,000 is being depreciated over five years. The franchise fee of $25,000 is being amortized over a period of five years as well. Note that the numbers are rounded off to the nearest dollar amount.)

3. When you subtract your total expenses from your gross profit, the remaining number is the net income or loss before taxes.

4. To do the second year P&L projections, simply project a realistic increase in sales (talk to present franchisees in the system for an estimated increase) and a corresponding increase in cost of sales. Expenditures will in some cases remain the same—rent, insurance and maybe advertising—and others such as payroll, royalty and telephone, may increase. In any case, make an informed judgment on these items, subtract the two figures, and you'll have net income or loss before taxes for the second year. Unless your circumstances are unusual, you'll be seeing a larger income or profit figure in the second year.

Why must you go through all these financial exercises? Though painstaking, they can show you whether the investment makes sound financial sense. If the numbers come out less than satisfactory and you go ahead anyway (maybe because you fall in love with the business), you may find yourself working long demanding hours with little in the way of salary or profit to show for it.

FINAL WORDS

Investigating a franchise opportunity is time consuming and may require some help from an accountant or other competent financial person. Unfortunately, I know of no shortcuts, but I do know that if you carefully follow the steps outlined in this chapter and act accordingly, you probably won't lose money in a franchise investment.

Figure 4.5 Franchise System Site Selection Worksheet

1. General Information:
    a. Site Location:
    Address:_____
    City:_____State:_____Zip:_____
    Frontage:_____Depth:_____Square Footage:_____
    Dimensions: Front:_____Rear:_____
                Left:_____Right:_____
    Tax Map and Tax Assessment Numbers:_____
    _____

    b. Seller/Landlord:
    Name:_____
    Tax ID#:_____
    Address:_____
    City:_____State:_____Zip:_____
    Telephone:(___)_____Fax:(___)_____

  c. Seller/Landlord's Attorney:

  Name:_____

  Address:_____

  City:_____State:_____Zip:_____

  Telephone:(___)_____Fax:(___)_____

  d. Listing Broker:

  Name:_____

  Address:_____

  City:_____State:_____Zip:_____

  Telephone:(___)_____Fax:(___)_____

  e. Surveyor/Engineer:

  Name:_____

  Address:_____

  City:_____State:_____Zip:_____

  Telephone:(___)_____Fax:(___)_____

2. Legal Data:

  a. Legal Description

  b. Covenants and Restrictions

3. Site Characteristics:

  a. Site Sketch

  b. Improvements

   (1) What improvements are on the site? Will demolition be required?

   (2) Does the site need cut or fill?

   (3) Will permits be needed for soil disturbance and erosion control?

c. Site Utility Data

Service Hook-Up	Line Size	On Site	Distance to
Gas	_____	_____	_____
Sewer	_____	_____	_____
Water	_____	_____	_____
Electrical	_____	_____	_____
Telephone	_____	_____	_____
Storm Sewer	_____	_____	_____

d. Site without Central Sewer and Water
Is a septic system permitted? If so, has the Health Department issued a permit for a septic system?

e. Storm Water Management
Does the jurisdiction require a storm water management plan, or can the site be surface drained? Must the run-off be held on-site?

f. Contaminated Soil
Has the site ever been used either as a gas station or for oil or chemical storage, a landfill, an auto salvage yard or similar use?

g. Easements
Will it be necessary to negotiate any easements external of the site?

h. The Subdivision Process
Will a subdivision, consolidated plat or similar work be required?

4. *Zoning:*
a. Current Zoning

b. Special Exceptions, Variances and Approvals
What is the estimated time to secure the requisite special exceptions, permits and approvals for a fast-food drive-thru restaurant?

5. Signage:

a. Freestanding Pole Signs

Is a freestanding pole sign permitted? How is the square footage of the sign's surface area calculated? What is the maximum permitted height of a freestanding pole sign?

b. Roof and Building Signs

Are roof signs that give the building corporate identity permitted? What factors govern the square footage of a sign's surface area then it is a part of the roof structure?

c. Off-Premise Signs and Highway Billboards

Are off-premise signs and billboards permitted?

6. Roadway and Traffic Data:

a. Primary Street

    (1) Number of traffic lanes and speed limit

    (2) One-way roadway or two-way

    (3) Daily traffic count—date taken and source

    (4) Traffic patterns and ingress and egress

b. Secondary Street

    (1) Number of traffic lanes and speed limit

    (2) One-way roadway or two-way

    (3) Daily traffic count—date taken and source

    (4) Traffic patterns and ingress and egress

c. Divider and Median Barriers

    (1) Does the roadway have a divider or median barrier?

    (2) What effect will the divider or median barrier have on access to the site?

    (3) Can crossovers be constructed? Outline the process and include estimated permit and construction costs.

    (4) What is the site's distance from existing crossovers?

(5) Are there any on-going or future changes planned for the road-way?

(6) What is the process for securing curb cuts into the site?

d. Deceleration/Acceleration Lanes

e. Roadway Sketch: show median strips, ingress and egress.

7. *Tax Data:*
   a. Special Assessments

   b. Tax Jurisdiction
   When are taxes due, and what are the tax account and tax map numbers of the proposed site?

8. *Educational Institutions (within three miles of proposed site):*

9. *Competitors (within three miles of proposed site):*
   National and Regional Competitors:
   Name:_____

   _____

   Distance from Site:_____

10. *Customer Generators:*
    a. Shopping Generators—Major Malls and Strip Centers:
    Name:_____

    _____

    Distance from Site:_____

    b. Major Employment Generators:
    Name:_____

    _____

    Distance from Site:_____

c. Other Generators and Draws—List all located within site's trade area.

11. *Financial Considerations:*

    a. Purchase Terms by Franchisor to Build for Franchisee's Use:

        (1) Purchase Price: $_____

        (2) Cost per Square Foot: $_____

        (3) Summary of Sale Terms and Conditions:_____

        _____

        _____

    b. Lease Terms:

        (1) Initial Base Rent: $_____

        (2) Periodic Increases (percentages): _____%

        (3) Fit-up Contributions, Site Work and Landlord Improvements:_____

        _____

        _____

        (4) Initial Term:____years

        Options Terms Exercisable for:_____

        Years at $_____per month

Carl Carlsson, FranchiseHelp Real Estate Division

5
WHAT THE UFOC TELLS YOU

The franchise system can be likened to a
cookbook. You may need to change the
recipes a little. But if you want to change it
entirely, you shouldn't buy the cookbook.
    RICK PETERSEN
    Interim Healthcare franchisee

In the previous chapter, you were told that each franchisor must produce a document called the Uniform Franchise Offering Circular (UFOC), which is submitted to the Federal Trade Commission. This document, with its 23 required items of information, is essential reading for any prospective franchisee.

Although the contents of the UFOC are prescribed, many franchisors will only present the minimum information needed to get by. So, to get an accurate assessment of the franchisor, you will need to do some reading between the lines and ask a lot of additional questions.

REQUIREMENTS FOR THE FRANCHISOR

The good news for prospective franchisees is that changes in UFOC guidelines, which were put into effect January 1, 1995, have greatly aided the cause of informing and protecting franchisees. Some of the major changes follow:

> *Litigation (Item 3).* The new guidelines have broadened the category appreciably. They now require that litigation reported include any action brought against the system by a present or former franchisee or by a supplier or landlord.

Tip

Read the litigation section carefully, looking especially for an excessive number of lawsuits by franchisees. That might indicate that a franchisor is not living up to its agreement. A red flag: franchisors that are involved in class action suits and/or expulsions from securities associations.

> *Initial Fees (Item 5).* Guidelines require that the average franchise fee paid in the prior fiscal year be disclosed if the initial franchise fee is not uniform.

Tip

This is your green light to negotiate fees. A record of non-uniform franchise fees indicates a willingness on the part of the franchisor to negotiate.

> *Initial Investment (Item 7).* Franchisors must disclose "all costs necessary to begin operation of the franchise and operate the franchise during the initial phase of the business." Second, franchisors must show how they arrived at these figures. Finally, three months will normally be considered the minimum reasonable period for the "initial phase" of operation.

Trap

Many franchisors have used one month of costs in initial phase estimates. Determine the actual time (i.e., one month, three months) the franchisor assigns to the initial phase. If the start-up time is underestimated, you will be underestimating the beginning costs as well.

Obligation to purchase or lease from approved sources or according to specifications (Item 8). Franchisors must disclose the total revenue generated by sales to franchisees, and the gross profit from those sales. All this information is to be taken from the franchisor's audited financial statements. Also, franchisors must make the criteria for approval of new suppliers and the necessary procedures available to franchisees.

Tip

Review this section to find out if the franchisor or approved source is charging franchisees a fair price for products or services. Look at the gross profit of the franchisor or approved source on required purchases and leases to see if it is reasonable.

Trap

Franchisors are often adamant about the franchisee's use of their approved suppliers. The prudent franchise investor should compare alternate supply sources with the franchisor's approved ones for price and quality.

Financing (Item 10). Franchisors must disclose not only the terms of financing offered by the franchise system, but also any financing arranged by the franchisor with banks and other lenders. In addition, franchisors are required to state interest using an annual percentage rate (APR) format. Finally, they must set a ceiling for any claim they would bring against a franchisee who defaults under a promissory note.

Tip

Franchisors that offer financial assistance to prospective franchisees provide a service. Just make sure that the terms and conditions of the system-sponsored financing are fair to the franchisee.

Franchisor's Obligations: advertising funds (Item 11). Franchisors must describe:

- ❧ How the various advertising funds (systemwide or regional) were actually spent, including the percentage of expenditure per category, in the most recently concluded fiscal year.

- ❧ Whether the franchisor or any of its affiliates receives any payments from these funds for providing goods or services to the funds.

- ❧ Whether the fund is audited and whether financial statements of the fund are available for review by the franchisee.

- ❧ Whether company-owned units must contribute to the funds and, if so, how much.

- ❧ Whether some franchisees are required to contribute at different rates than others.

- ❧ The percentage of the advertising fund spent on advertising that is principally a solicitation for the sale of new franchises.

Tip

When you examine a company's advertising program and strategy, look for clear-cut goals and effective use of funding. You don't want to find out that most of the advertising dollars go toward attracting new franchisees, not customers.

Franchisor's Obligations: computer databases (Item 11). With almost all companies now using computer technology, franchisors must disclose information about the company hardware and software systems—in non-technical language. This includes disclosure of the principal functions of the database, its technical specifications, the types and amount of data on the system, the cost to the franchisee for access to the system, anticipated tele-communications charges, costs of upgrades, the franchisor's experience operating a computer network, whether software is custom or off-the-shelf, the amount of user support, how often the system is updated, and how often the system was "down" due to operating problems in the preceding fiscal year.

Franchisor's Obligations: operating manual (Item 11). In the UFOC franchisors must include the table of contents from their operating manual. Also, they will state the number of pages devoted to each subject and the total number of pages in the manual.

Trap

The operating manual is the blueprint of the business. Be alert to systems that do not have extensive manuals for guiding franchisees.

Financial Statements (Item 21). Franchisors are now required to provide a two-year comparative format that includes not only balance sheets and income statements, but also statements of operations, stockholders' equity and cash flows.

In the nearly five years since the adoption of the present UFOC directives, the Franchise Committee of the North American Securities Administrators Association (NASAA) has identified additional issues in the UFOC items for clarification and interpretation. October 31, 1998 was the close of the comment period regarding 1998 additions. The 1998 comments are likely to be adopted largely in their current form and will be used by franchisors in their preparation of the UFOC.

Below are several of the comments which should be of interest to a prospective franchisee. Note that the comments are presented in a question and answer format.

Item 1: Predecessor/Change of Ownership
Question: If control of a franchisor changes, is a former controlling owner a predecessor?
Answer: A change in ownership of a franchisor does not necessarily mean that the former owner is a "predecessor." A former owner must be disclosed as a predecessor only if the franchisor acquired the majority of its assets (calculated as of the date of acquisition) from that former owner.

Item 2: Employment History
Question: Must the employment history of a person identified in Item 2 be limited to five years?
Answer: Employment history should be limited to five years. However, a longer period may be permissible if the extended employment history is relevant to the franchise being offered.

Item 5: Fee Disclosure
Question: If a franchisor occasionally sells company-owned outlets to franchisees, does the purchase price of the outlets constitute an initial franchise fee and, if so, must it be disclosed in Item 5 and on the cover page?
Answer: If an isolated occurrence, the cover page need not reflect the purchase price. However, Item 5 should disclose these

occasional sales during the preceding fiscal year and the range of amounts involved.

Item 6: Uniformity

Question: Must a franchisor disclose whether each continuing fee is uniform?

Answer: A franchisor must disclose whether any continuing fees currently being charged are uniform. It need not disclose that fees charged in prior periods are different from the current fees.

Item 8: Multiple Brands

Question: If a franchisor has multiple branded outlets, should it separate each brand's revenue in Item 8?

Answer: A franchisor generally should segregate brand revenues. If it is impractical or unreasonable to segregate revenue by brand, a franchisor is not required to do so as long as it clearly discloses this fact.

Trap

Many large, diversified companies that franchise do not segregate brand revenues. Although it is often possible to assess the general financial health of the parent company, the lack of financial information about a particular franchise brand forces a potential investor to extrapolate the brand's strength in sometimes obscure ways. As noted above, the 1998 guidelines will not require that the franchisor provide this information.

Item 10: Financing Terms

Question: If financing is offered on an individually negotiated basis or on widely varying forms, what documents must be attached to the UFOC?

Answer: If there is no standard form, Item 10 itself or an exhibit must disclose the material terms of the various financing.

Item 11: Computers

Question: How much detailed information must be disclosed about computer hardware and software?

Answer: The disclosure must contain enough information to allow the prospective franchisee to comparison shop the items involved. If computer system components change frequently, an amendment is necessary only if a material cost item or a material change in cost is involved.

THE FRANCHISE AGREEMENT

In the first chapter of this book, we noted the fact that you are not in actuality "buying" a franchise. The transaction is closer to a lease agreement. Bret Lowell, a franchise attorney with Rudnick, Wolfe, Epstein and Zeidman in Washington, DC, characterizes it in a slightly different way. Lowell says you are "often buying a limited opportunity" with an initial duration of five years or ten years, which may then go through two or three renewals. He did agree, however, that in many regards, it is like a lease. The franchise agreement discusses fees, terms, renewals, termination and other elements found in most leases.

When you sign the franchise agreement, you have agreed to make payments and assume obligations in exchange for the use of a trade name and logo and a demonstrated formula for success. The franchise operating manual contains the formula. This manual should cover everything the franchisee needs to know to do business. It documents the standards and policies that all franchisees are to follow. The manual is "loaned" to the franchisee for the term of the franchise agreement. Upon the expiration or termination of the agreement, the book must be returned to the franchisor.

Is Anything in the Agreement Negotiable?

There is very little latitude for change in most franchising agreements. "Historically, the franchise systems have said that the agreement can't be changed because then the disclosure document won't match up," says Bret Lowell. Continuing, he adds, "A negotiated change that benefits the franchisee and doesn't challenge the disclosure document [UFOC] is now okay."

Lisa Brumm, a Formals Etc. franchisee (rented formal wear) felt that because her chosen franchise was at a very early stage, some things should be negotiable. She had heard franchisors claiming they couldn't change things in the contract on a case-by-case basis because they would have to re-register with the state if they did. Lisa's advice: "Don't believe this. Check with the proper state officials. In many cases changes are permitted."

Her position is verified by Bret Lowell. He sees more negotiating on contract points going on now. He has found that "a prospective franchisee can negotiate more with a brand new franchisor." He also notes that a franchisee who is considered "a big player"—i.e., someone who is going to buy multiple units or a large region—will have some clout and be able to negotiate more points. "However," Lowell is quick to point out, "there is a limit as to how far the franchise system will bend. They won't allow you to change things that challenge uniformity or economies of scale, for example. They say if we do it for you, we'll have to do it for everyone."

Tip

Most major points of the franchise agreement will not be negotiated by the franchisor, so if there's something you cannot live with, be ready to walk away from the deal.

"Franchisees need to realize that they're not getting involved in a one-to-one relationship," says Bret Lowell. Franchisors strive to keep everything uniform and shy away from making exceptions. The reasoning behind this is easy to understand. An exception for one franchisee can set a precedent for the entire system. This factor, however, should not keep you from requesting changes, but it should help you to set priorities and to negotiate only for those points that make or break the deal for you.

FRANCHISE FEES AND ROYALTIES

Just about all franchisors require the franchisee to pay a franchise fee. It is the payment for admission and training in the franchisor's organized business system. The fee may be required in one lump sum or in installments and can range from a low of about $3,000 to over $100,000. The majority of franchise fees seem to fall around the $20,000–$25,000 range per unit. If you are buying a large territory or region, you can expect a franchise fee that exceeds $100,000.

Tip

Be very sure you've settled on the right franchise, because, once you have paid the fee, it's doubtful you will get it back if you change your mind. Most fees are non-refundable.

Trap

Don't be enticed by a franchisor's very low franchise fee. Find out what it covers. If training, support and marketing aren't included in the initial fee, you can end up paying much more on a piecemeal basis than you would with a higher fee that includes all these things.

In addition to an initial franchise fee, there is generally an on-going fee called a royalty. This is usually payable monthly or weekly, based on a percentage of gross sales. This payment covers the use of a trademark and tradename, as well as continuing services, which include training programs, marketing and sales materials, construction and start-up assistance, site selection, new product development, newsletters and regional and national meetings.

Tip

Be very careful with royalty fees that are paid on a weekly basis. Work this through in your cash flow projections. You don't want to be in the position of having to pay the franchisor before you have actually collected the funds.

Royalty fees vary widely by franchisor and by industry. In our research, we have found that a majority of franchisees pay in the 5–6% of gross sales range. However, we also find franchisees paying 10% or more, and some paying no royalty at all! These two extremes are certainly in the minority.

Franchisees who do not pay a royalty are, for the most part, in businesses where the franchisee buys on-going services and products from the franchisor. Some such businesses include Leadership Management (franchisee buys programming materials), Money Mailer (printing services from franchisor) and Citizens Against Crime (franchisor provides products for sale).

To be sure, in many systems, a franchisee must buy products and services from the franchisor and still pay a royalty fee. In the case of a franchise with no royalty fee, a royalty can be captured in the obligatory product or service price.

If your chosen franchise has a 10% or higher royalty fee, find out exactly what you are getting for your money. The best course of action is to compare the franchisor's royalty fee to other franchise systems in the same industry. If other franchisors (in a similar business) are not charging an equivalent fee, then the management of the higher priced franchise should give you a very specific justification for its higher royalty.

Tip

Ask yourself this question when considering a royalty fee (especially one that seems high in comparison to other franchisors): Does the franchise have such powerful name recognition that the high royalty is warranted?

Another variant you may find with royalty payments is that some are paid on a sliding scale. Usually these start at a number like 5 or 6% and can rise as high as 15% as gross sales increase. In these instances, you will need to do some careful calculations to make sure that the profit from increasing sales doesn't all end up going to the franchisor in royalty payments instead of to your bottom line.

Tip

Find out if franchisees are paying their royalties. It spells trouble if they aren't. Either they're not doing well enough to pay the fee or they're not satisfied with the franchisor's support and service.

Advertising Fees

Advertising fees, like royalty fees, vary from franchisor to franchisor and industry to industry. The fee can be a percentage of your gross sales or a flat fee paid on a monthly basis. Advertising fees usually range between 2–5% of gross sales.

Many franchisors of a certain size with, say, 500 operating units or more, divide the advertising fee into two parts. The first is a system-wide advertising fee, while the second is used for local or regional advertising through an advertising co-operative formed with other franchisees in the region.

Some questions that you should ask the franchisor about its advertising include:

1. How much of the fee is spent for national advertising? How will this portion be spent?

2. Is any of the advertising fee used for administrative purposes? If so, how much?

3. Are audited figures on advertising expenditures available to franchisees?

4. Are advertising materials, such as camera-ready art, circulars, direct mail pieces and posters provided to franchisees? Is there a cost?

5. Is there any input from franchisees on the use of advertising dollars?

Almost all the franchisors that do not levy advertising fees are in the start-up phase or are young franchise systems where a national advertising program hasn't yet been established. Franchisees are expected to do their own local advertising and usually the franchisor will stipulate that a 1 or 2% of gross sales budget be allocated to local advertising. National advertising fee structures are usually written into the UFOC, to be put into effect at the franchisor's discretion. This normally happens when the system becomes large enough to make national advertising a worthwhile expenditure.

Tip

National advertising cannot be effective for a franchise system unless a critical mass of franchisees is located throughout the United States. If the system has few units and they are widely scattered, then only local advertising will be cost effective.

In the course of preparing evaluation reports of franchise concepts at FranchiseHelp, we talk to many franchisees at a great variety of franchise systems. But there is one thing we can almost routinely rely on—complaints about the franchisor's advertising program. As this seems to be the number one complaint of franchisees across the board, your chosen franchisor's advertising program is an area that should be well researched.

To be sure, there are still many franchisees satisfied with the franchisor's use of their advertising dollars. Most of these tend to be fast-food franchisees associated with well-known systems such as Wendy's and Pizza Hut. These franchisees notice a huge surge in business each time a new, national advertising campaign appears.

For those franchisees not happy with the franchisor advertising, the complaints are somewhat the same, whatever the company. Perhaps these comments from disgruntled franchisees will help you in posing your questions to the franchisor.

"All they do is give out more and more coupons and I am not redeeming some. Why? Because some are for 99 cents and it costs me more than that. I don't want to lose money."
An ice cream franchisee

"We give them 1% and they give us table tents [point of purchase materials]."
A deli franchisee

"The company takes our one percent for the national advertising fund but I have no idea what they do with it because we don't have national advertising. They say it defrays the cost of local advertising. It comes back in the form of flyers and ---- like that."
A deli franchisee

"The franchisor has all these different contracts and a store 40 miles away doesn't contribute to the marketing. We pay 7.5% and I feel the advertising is extremely inefficient and offers no benefit."
A fast-food franchisee from a system that has older stores on a different contract which pay no advertising fees

FRANCHISOR TRAINING AND SUPPORT

Virtually every franchise system offers a training program to new franchisees. This is vital because there's a good chance that the franchisee will be new to the industry. Only about a quarter of the franchise systems require previous experience in the industry. These are predominantly in businesses that require a very specialized knowledge or skill, for example, optical products and services, accounting and tax services, real estate services and some restaurant systems. In any case, getting trained in the particulars of the franchisor's system is essential.

The franchise agreement should spell out all initial and continuing training obligations of the franchisor in detail. You should also query the franchisor about the following:

1. Is previous or related experience necessary to operate the franchise?

2. Is training optional, recommended or mandatory?

3. What is the nature and extent of the training?

4. What are the costs, and who is responsible for paying? Do these costs include classroom training, lodging, meals and transportation?

5. Where is the location of the training facilities?

6. Is the training of employees included in any training cost charge?

7. Will there be a continuing training program?

8. Will there be video or audio tapes or mailed written materials? Is there a charge?

9. Is start-up assistance provided for pre-opening and for a time after opening?

Tip

If the franchisor allows it, sit in on a training session before you buy the franchise.

What to Expect from Training

In our survey of franchisees, all said they had attended a training program of one kind or another. Training ranges in time from two to three days all the way up to eight weeks or more. The longer stints are associated with those businesses that require a specialized skill or technical training or one of the very standardized fast-food operations. The average training time is one to two weeks. The trend is to extend the training period across the board. Apparently, franchisors have listened to their franchisees who complained of too short a training period.

For example, Larry Gambino, a Priority Management franchise (management skills program) was trained over eight years ago at company headquarters in Vancouver, BC. He recalls that it was adequate then, but says the training program is now much improved. He also benefits from the new on-going training, which is led by regional coaches. They meet with franchisees once a month to help keep them on track and maintain a focus on building the business.

FranchiseHelp analysts recently spoke to two franchisees, both in the auto aftermarket business. Their comments on the two respective training programs illustrate potential problem areas. One franchisee said, "I've been in the automotive business for thirty years, so I knew what I was getting into. But the training is pretty good; they've changed it to be more office-oriented than shop-oriented. An owner doesn't have to know how to change brake pads. If the owner can't do it, he will have to find someone who can."

The other franchisee had several complaints about his training program. He said, "The training is not as thorough as I would have liked it to be. They don't provide us with the details of the business, such as inventory. Their aim is to bring in business people, not transmission people, and then they want us to sell parts, but don't tell us how to organize that part of the business."

Tip

Ken Dykhuis, a Mighty Distributing Co. franchisee (auto parts distribution), spent two weeks in the Atlanta corporate headquarters for training. When asked if the training was sufficient, Ken said, "You can always use more training, but at some point you just have to go out and do it."

The majority of franchisors include the cost of training for the purchaser, and usually one or two employees in the initial fee. There's less consensus regarding room, board and transportation, but, in general, franchisees pay these expenses out of their own pockets.

The classroom training sessions are usually held at the corporate headquarters. In polling franchisees, most assert that they could have used more training in administration, especially in the computer systems. In addition to the classroom sessions, many franchisees also get on-the-job training held at company-owned units or other franchisee units. This experience may be followed by on-site training and support, with most systems sending one or two company representatives to help franchisees through the early stages of their openings.

Jeff Grayson, a Pizzeria Uno franchisee, had lots of prior experience in the restaurant business, but even so, Grayson says, "I trained up in Framingham, Massachusetts, for eight weeks, and it was well worth it. You're responsible for 50–100 employees. The first restaurant opening is very tough, but subsequent stores are easier because then you can mix in some experienced employees with the new ones."

Buying into a new franchise system is likely to be a totally different experience. Ken Wisotzky was the first My Favorite Muffin (retail muffins) franchisee, with only one company-owned store opened. There was no formal training program set up, so Ken got his training by working at the company store for a little over a week. The major problem, according to Wisotzky, was "that it seemed like a very easy operation," but he didn't realize then that the location had a relatively low-volume business. When he opened

117

his own business, he found that he had more than double the number of customers. This meant he immediately needed additional employees and he also had to change some operational techniques to compensate for the greater volume of business.

On the positive end, the training program can pay some unexpected dividends. Take the experience of George Colgate, a VR Business Brokers (sales of small businesses) franchisee. Colgate trained for two weeks in the training center in Dallas. The first week he learned about business broker-age, and the second week concentrated on office management. As part of the training, new franchisees are put out on the street and have to make a cold call to see how it feels. This experience actually got George's business off to a great start. During training, he managed to list a business and to sell a business.

Sample Training Programs

Depending upon the type of business that is being franchised, the training program can be highly formalized or informal or somewhere in-between. Training can take five or six days or even a year or more, but most likely it will be about one to three weeks.

The following descriptions will give you an idea how some franchisors structure their training programs.

- *Training for Pearle Vision Store franchisees:* The franchisee and the operator must complete a 90-day program called Phase One. In addition, all employees involved with the franchised business must successfully complete this training program within 90 days of commencing employment. Phase One training materials are provided free of cost and the program is an in-store training process. The content of the training focuses on fundamental technical sales and service techniques, as well as retail and lab procedures. After a proprietary computer system is purchased from the franchisor, the company will provide the franchisee and the business operator with system training, either at the franchisee's location (for a charge of $250 per day plus any company representative expenses) or at a central training location where the franchisee and any number of employees may attend for a one-time charge of $1,000. All travel and other expenses are borne by the franchisee.

    Training for A&W Restaurants: Before opening the restaurant, either the franchisee or the designated restaurant manager will be required to attend an initial training program. The training class is an integration of both classroom instruction and on-the-job training. The class meets six days per week for the first two weeks, followed by four consecutive days in the third week. Training takes place at the company training facilities in the Detroit, MI, area and covers the entire operating procedure for the restaurant. There is no charge for the program, but the franchisee will be responsible for all other costs, such as travel and hotel.

THE QUALITY OF FRANCHISOR SUPPORT

In the course of research for this book and other interviews with franchisees for FranchiseHelp, we have found that the quality of franchisor support is generally good. Almost all systems respond quickly to franchisee questions and will help to solve problems; some franchisees even get calls from the corporate office to help morale when they are experiencing a down day.

Most franchisees also agree, however, that help and advice in running the day-to-day business is where the support stops. When queried about the kind of support available if they were to sustain financial troubles, most franchisees feel they are on their own. Some systems do have a program in place that will deal with a franchisee's more serious concerns. For example, a franchisee of Round Table Pizza (a regional system) told us about a type of task force the company can deploy. He said, "If a store isn't doing well, they can ask for assistance and someone from corporate will be sent to look it over. For example, if a competitor comes in across the street, the representative will advise on moves and countermoves in terms of marketing and advertising."

FRANCHISEES WITH A VOICE

A franchise advisory board made up of franchisees is fairly standard except for the start-up franchises. The quality of these boards varies. They may be rubber stamps of the franchisor philosophy or they may be independent-thinking boards that really effect change.

For most systems this advisory concept is just finding its way, and its effectiveness will improve as more and more franchisees voice their opinions.

In our interviews, we found that at least 50% of franchisees don't even know if there is a franchisee advisory board or council for their franchise and, if they are aware of an existing board, they often have a very fuzzy notion of what the board is doing. Franchisees who are knowledgeable about these councils, however, often have strong opinions about their make up and effectiveness. For example, one IHOP franchisee didn't like the chosen board members because "you wind up voting for guys who are usually multi-unit owners and end up with the same people over and over. In my opinion, they don't speak out for the little guys." One Dairy Queen franchisee lauded the efforts of their franchisee board because the members "were really fighting for the franchisees and had succeeded in lowering prices [franchisor-controlled] for toppings and hamburgers which are now cheaper than ten years ago."

When evaluating a franchise opportunity, look for systems where franchisees are encouraged to voice their opinions and to suggest improvements, rather than simply follow the rules. It is also critical that the franchisor has a support system in place that is able to respond not only to start-up problems, but also to those encountered by the franchisee in the second, third and subsequent years.

Term of Agreement, Renewal and Termination

The term of agreement is the number of years the franchisee may operate the business. When the term expires, the right and license to operate the business will end. Of course, many agreements provide for renewal rights, so that a franchisee has the option of extending the term of the contract.

Tip

Check the agreement carefully to see if the franchisor imposes a renewal fee. You may also be required to renew under the terms of the franchisor's prevailing franchise agreement, leaving you open to the possibility of higher royalties and advertising fees in the future.

Most franchise terms fall into the five to ten year range. Bret Lowell, a franchise attorney, noted that sometimes franchisors impose shorter terms so that they can "assess the business on an on-going basis." He says that, "Businesses change, technologies change and sometimes the original franchisee is no longer right for the business. That's why many franchisors prefer to go with three five-year term contracts instead of one 15-year term." On a positive note, Lowell has found that most franchise contracts are renewed.

An attorney can help you review the franchisor's provisions for renewal and termination. It is very important that you determine, with your attorney, what specific conditions must be met for renewal and the circumstances that could lead to termination of the agreement before its expiration.

Tip

Hire a franchise attorney to look over your franchise investment and participate in negotiations with the franchisor. One franchisee said she didn't want to hire a general attorney whom she'd be paying to learn about the franchise business.

You'll also want to consider and evaluate the franchisor's termination processes. Some of the questions you need answered are:

1. What are the defaults for which there may be a termination?

2. Are you given notice of a default and a reasonable amount of time to remedy it?

3. Does the franchisor have any option to cancel the agreement other than for "good cause"?

4. Under what conditions (if any) is the franchisee able to cancel the agreement?

5. If the franchisee is not renewed or terminated, does the franchisor have a responsibility to buy back any equipment, inventory or other assets?

6. If there is an obligation to buy back franchisee assets, what are the purchase terms? Is there an independent appraisal?

7. Does the franchisor have the right to take over your lease upon termination?

Trap

Check the agreement carefully for high sales quotas or high minimum inventory purchases. Not meeting these goals could result in termination of the franchise agreement.

The franchise agreement may also include a non-compete clause in the termination section. This clause will prevent a franchisee from competing in the same business for a period of years if the franchise business is terminated. Try to negotiate an agreement that excludes a non-compete covenant. As an example, a franchisee we interviewed in the photography business chose a franchise with a standard five-year non-compete clause. However, since the franchisee's entire business background had been in photography, he couldn't accept this condition. His attorney managed to have this clause deleted. If the franchisor won't budge on this point, you must carefully assess the risks and costs you will face if the franchise fails and you must leave the industry.

EXCLUSIVE RIGHTS TO TERRITORIES AND AREAS

Most franchisees have very loose arrangements, if any at all, regarding territorial rights for their franchises. Many franchisees interviewed said their territorial rights were not spelled out in writing, but that they had arrived at a verbal agreement that they accepted in good faith. This is not a very secure arrangement from either a legal or a financial standpoint.

Franchisor reticence to spell out the territory and exclusive area rights of franchisees in the franchise agreement has caused widespread discontent among franchisees. Let's examine some of the common ways franchisors approach the question of territorial rights and see what you can do to prevent potential problems.

Tip

Here's a question to ask the franchisor: "What guarantees do I have that a company-owned outlet or a new franchisee will not encroach on my marketing area?"

123

Defining Exclusivity

Depending on the business, there are all kinds of ways to define a territory. Sometimes, areas are defined by population ratios. For instance, one business service franchisee says there are no exclusive territories in his system and he finds that this causes problems. A franchise is assigned for each 250,000 population. Consequently, many franchisees service metro areas and can end up overlapping and competing with one another.

In other cases, the franchisee may be assigned specific accounts. Here the boundaries are a little clearer, except in some instances, where one franchisee can go into another franchisee's territory to sell a large account, if the decision maker is based in the first franchisee's territory.

Zip codes are yet another way that territories are defined. Decorating Den, for instance, uses boundaries defined by zip codes. When a customer calls into the main office, however, from an area which is not in an assigned zip code, those calls are given to franchisees on a rotating basis. The Pressed 4 Time franchise is another system which is governed by zip codes; 30,000 prime clients is considered a territory.

Protected Territories

The "protected territory" approach is a little more nebulous and is rarely written into the agreement. It is usually little more than an unwritten understanding between the franchisor and franchisee. Here are some typical franchisee situations:

> ࿔ A photo store owner initially had a three-mile radius that was exclusive to his store. Now the radius around newer units has become smaller, and some stores are competing for the same business.

    ❧ Another retail franchisee has an unwritten three-mile radius rule between stores that has already been breached by the franchisor.

Sometimes territories are clearly stipulated and enforced. For example, Lisa Brumm, a Formal Etc. franchise, has an exclusive territory spanning 25 miles. If any other prospective franchisee wants to open a shop there, she or he would have to pay Lisa a royalty. Also, her agreement allows for a larger "protected territory" where she has "first right of refusal" should a store open up.

Trap

Oral representations rarely hold up in court. If it's important to you, get it in writing.

Sometimes territorial rights carry with them certain obligations, especially if you are buying into a fairly large area. For example, Jeff Grayson, a Pizzeria Uno franchisee, has territorial rights to a large area around Orlando, FL. In return for those rights, he has to open a certain number of restaurants in a limited period of time. And, if Arny Grushkin, a Unishippers franchisee with an exclusive territory, does not uphold the performance standard in his franchise agreement then Unishippers can buy back his franchise.

SELECTING A SITE

Site selection, as we have said earlier, can be critically important to the success of the franchise, especially where heavy customer traffic is necessary. If the site or location of the business is important, the franchisor should help to select a site. At the least, the franchisor should have criteria and guidelines to assist you in your site selection. Some of the guidelines used for selection are: trade area population, demographics, traffic patterns, competition, industry and office space and visibility of signage. Often the franchisor has already identified and purchased a real estate site, and then started looking for the franchisee.

If the franchise management does not offer you advice or show a great deal of expertise in site selection—beware! After all, part of what you're paying for is the franchisor's experience at determining what will be a successful site. The franchisor should have a proven location standard in order to assist you.

Tip

If you are considering an urban location for your business, factor the following costs into your decision making: you will need to secure a business license, adhere to zoning require-ments, and probably use union workers for any building improvements. Also, consider the increased expense of insurance and security.

Some questions to ask are:

1. Who finds the site? Who negotiates the lease or purchases/ builds the facility.

2. If the franchisor has already picked out a site, what variables were considered to make the decision?

3. Will the franchisor obtain and "build-out" a site and then sub-lease it to you? What are the terms?

4. If the franchisee is to develop the site, are the plans and specifi-cations provided? Does the initial fee cover this cost?

BUYING A PREVIOUSLY-OWNED FRANCHISE

Let's suppose you are interested in buying a resale franchise. You will be purchasing the franchise from the present franchisee, but you will still have to sign an agreement with the franchisor, so the contents of the UFOC are still equally important to you. Besides the agreed upon purchase price with the franchisee, often you will be asked to pay a transfer fee to the franchise system. In the case of one franchisee we talked to, it was one-third the current franchise fee.

The price of a resale franchise is usually higher than a new franchise bought from the franchisor, because you will be buying a customer base, equipment and the goodwill of an operating business. How then do you determine if the franchise is priced fairly? We asked George Colgate at VR Business Brokers how a prospective buyer should evaluate the value of a resale franchise. Colgate says that on-going businesses are often priced according to this formula: one year's net profit, plus inventory value, plus fixtures and equipment value, plus real estate value (if applicable), plus goodwill. The dollar amount assigned to goodwill is defined as the favor or prestige that a business has acquired beyond the mere value of what it sells.

Colgate also suggests that the buyer should analyze the cash flow of the business by studying the owner's financial records. The prospective buyer should determine if the following three goals can be met:

1. A return on investment (consistent with today's market conditions) on the down payment and start-up capital. (The reasoning here is that you could be receiving interest on the monies invested in the business, so you would expect at least a conservative return on this investment money.)

2. The throw-off of enough cash to service the debt and eventually retire it.

3. A payment of a reasonable wage to the owner-operator.

Tip

You may have to arrange a different type of training program with the franchisor if you buy a resale franchise. A case in point is Mike Bueti, a Merry Maids (residential cleaning) franchisee. He found that one week's training provided by the franchisor was not sufficient because he had inherited 19 employees and established accounts through the resale. He didn't have the option of learning as he went along as most franchisees do as they develop their business. Bueti had to hit the ground running to keep the on-going business running smoothly.

Buying a previously-owned franchise is becoming a viable option for more and more investors. Assuming the business is reasonably successful, here are some of the reasons for the increasing popularity of this choice:

- *Faster Profits and Cash Flow to the Owner.* Since there are no real start-up costs and the business is on-going, you should see a profit and draw a salary almost immediately.

- *Simplified Planning.* Projections are easier to make because you have historical records as a basis for financial and market forecasting.

- *Expedited Financing.* Often the previous owner will accept a down payment, followed by monthly payments until the agreed upon price is covered. The new owner will not have to seek financing from lending institutions or private investors.

- *Built-In Advantages.* The new owner will usually inherits experienced employees, established suppliers and loyal customers.

If you'd like to explore the idea of buying a previously-owned business, you have to know where to look to find them. Here are four suggestions:

1. If you're settled on a particular franchise, talk to other franchisees. They often know about resales within the system.

2. Talk to the franchisor.

3. Look for advertisements in local and national newspapers.

4. Find a business broker who specializes in franchises. These brokers are paid by percentage commissions on the completed sales. Commissions are usually paid by the seller of the business.

As you may have guessed, not all resales are good deals. Look out for resales where antiquated facilities and inventory are calculated into the purchase price. You may have to add additional monies to modernize the facilities and replace the inventory. The biggest problem, though, may be encountered if you buy a franchise which has been allowed to deteriorate. You may be inheriting the ill will of the customers, and retrieving alienated customers will be very difficult and costly.

Tip

Here's some good advice from Jeanette Fuller, who bought a Tutor Time Learning Center resale with her husband. She says, "If you are buying a resale—especially one that is in difficulty—negotiate so that the franchisor will be obliged to buy back the franchise if it is not successful in a certain amount of time."

FINAL WORDS

By the time you have carefully read the Uniform Franchise Offering Circular and received the necessary professional advice, there should be little left to investigate in the agreement and no real surprises. If, however, you find yourself uneasy and strongly opposed to several stipulations of the franchise agreement, get ready to move on to another opportunity.

6
What the UFOC Doesn't Tell You

No doubt about it, the franchisor's Uniform Franchise Offering Circular is a valuable and informative document, but only if the prospective franchisee takes the time and effort to carefully read and analyze it. There are, however, some items that are barely touched upon in this document that are crucial to the discovery process. This chapter highlights other topics that need closer investigation.

Industry Outlook

Prospective franchisees should evaluate the industry in which the franchise business participates. Is the industry growing, declining or maintaining the status quo? What factors impact the industry's health? What do forecasters and industry pundits predict for the near term? The longer term? Granted, this information is not always readily available. Nevertheless, accurate industry statistics are essential to the decision-making process. To fine-tune what may only be gut-feelings, ask the franchisor for information and statistics on the industry, or use the Internet or your local library for research. The point is that you don't want to license a franchise in an industry that is in a steep decline or is being reconfigured with a number of shake-outs expected.

At my company, FranchiseHelp, we routinely look at the industry in which a franchise operates when evaluating a specific opportunity. For example, a recent auto aftermarket industry evaluation might look something like this:

> The parts-and-services business is the most profitable component of the auto industry and is estimated to be a $500 billion a year business. There are more cars on the road than ever before. The replacement parts category of the automobile industry includes such items as spark plugs, brake pads, batteries, oil and gas filters, shock absorbers, struts, transmissions, exhaust systems and air filters. Replacement parts are sold through specialized repair shops, general repair shops, dealers, service stations, auto parts stores, discount stores and auto do-it-yourself shops. Industry experts expect the industry to maintain a moderate, long-term demand growth rate. Industry consolidation will most likely result in the further disappearance of family-owned parts businesses, allowing the name players to garner a larger share of the industry.

Auto Repair Trends
1. Car owners are keeping their vehicles longer. The average age of cars on the road in 1994 was 8.2 years. This hurts new car demand, but increases sales of replacement parts and tires.

2. The number of cars and light trucks on the road continues to increase. There are 175–200 million of these vehicles on the high-

ways, and this should mean more maintenance and repair business.

3. Automotive technology has become too complex for most do-it-yourselfers. Car owners will seek reliable, expert help for repairs.

4. Traditional service stations are declining in number. An estimated 75% of consumer gasoline is now sold through self-service outlets so the trusted, local auto mechanic is not available to repair cars so readily.

As another example, a report on the floral industry would include information such as the following:

The floral industry has changed dramatically over the past 15 years. The changes have been primarily in the volume of flowers sold and in the distribution of the flowers. Since the industry is so fragmented, the gross sales of the industry are not currently available, but anecdotal evidence is strong that the industry is growing rapidly. Customers no longer view buying flowers as the luxury item that they once did.

The manner in which flowers are brought to the public has also changed substantially. Whereas flowers were once available almost exclusively in florist shops, today flowers can be purchased through large network services, grocery stores, street vendors and even on the Internet.

In the 1960s, the florist who wanted to send an arrangement to another town would call a florist that she or he knew. Later, many florists banded together to form an association to make this practice easier and more efficient. It also helped to guarantee that the product they sent was of uniform quality. The sending florist received a premium for sending the arrangement over the system (usually 20% of the order's value) and the receiving florist would then make the arrangement for its full value and would consider the 20% "commission" a cost of doing business.

Now there are a variety of ways to send flowers to another location. Some people use an 1-800 number, such as 1-800-FLOW-ERS, to reach a floral service that must spend advertising dollars for the 800 number. Others may use florists who in turn use the various wire services, such as FTD, Teleflora or AFS, to send the flowers. A service charge is added to the price of the flowers to pay for this accommodation.

MARKET STRENGTH AND COMPETITION

Unfortunately, the UFOC does not include an assessment of the company's market position or that of its competitors, both of which are crucial pieces of information. Officers of the franchise system should be able to give you a pretty good idea of how the company fares relative to its competition. In most cases, though, you should go beyond what the franchisor tells you and do some investigation and research on your own.

Trap

Find out the franchisor's marketing plans. Ask if it now sells or plans to sell products or services through a distribution channel other than the franchisees. For example, a franchisor might sell its products through a grocery chain and end up competing with its franchisees.

If your intended business is a restaurant, make a point of consulting *Nation's Restaurant News,* which publishes an annual (usually in June or July) two-issue survey of all the major restaurant concepts. The survey includes numbers and rankings as to market share and other key indicators. Many of the other major industries have industry-specific newsletters and magazines that track the market participants. Contact the editorial staff of these publications and inquire whether a survey or ranking of market participants is available.

Briefly, let's look at an example in the restaurant business, Taco John's, to get an idea of the type of information you should gather.

Taco John's (TJ) is a fast-food Mexican restaurant. In the broadest sense, it competes in the very crowded and highly contested group called "sandwich chains." This category is dominated by giants like McDonald's, Burger King and Wendy's. TJ does not compare in number of units or in system-wide sales to these market leaders, although in the more limited category of Mexican fast-food, Taco John's fares much better. In spite of the fact that it is currently a regional chain (mostly Western and Midwestern states), Taco John's is the third largest Mexican quick-service chain in the country. The first in the category is Tricon Global Restaurants, Inc. which owns Taco Bell.

Direct competition for Taco John's includes the Mexican fast-food leader Taco Bell, as well as Del Taco, El Pollo Loco, Taco Cabana and the new Fresh Mex concepts. While Taco Bell is far and away the leader, more targeted competition is in the Second 100 chains as ranked by *Nation's Restaurant News*. In this group, Del Taco posts 1997 sales of $238 million, A&W Restaurants at $194.6 million and Taco John's sales are $174 million. (Go on to look at primary competitors and what they're doing.)

Tip

Check in the UFOC to see if the principals have the experience necessary to manage and operate the franchise system. If you are serious about the franchise, you will visit the franchise headquarters and meet the management in person. At this time you can get a further impression of the management's level of competency.

CURRENT FINANCIAL CONDITION OF THE FRANCHISOR

In Item 21 of the UFOC, franchisors are required to submit balance sheets, income statements and other financial data. Ascertain whether the franchisor is a public or private company. Often a franchising company is owned by a parent company, which is very large and has a very complicated corporate structure with a number of affiliates. The potential franchisee has to be able to sift through the material to determine the financial strength of the franchisor. It is highly recommended that you have an accountant or franchise consulting service assist you with this task. (See Chapter 8 for some potential problems for franchisees that might result from a franchisor's shaky financial position.)

Tip

If your chosen franchise is a subsidiary of a larger company, find out if the parent company stands behind the franchisor financially.

An indication of a company's liquidity or solvency is the relationship of current assets to current liabilities. This is called the current ratio. For example, let's assume that the ratio is 3.24:1 at the company's last prepared balance sheet date. This means there are $3.24 of current assets to satisfy every $1.00 of current liabilities. Generally speaking, a ratio of 2:1 or greater is an indication of adequate liquidity. However, in some businesses, such as a restaurant operation, enough cash can be collected on a daily basis to replenish the checking account. Thus, a ratio a little under 2:1 may not be as serious as it would be as for a manufacturer or retailer of big ticket items. Check the current ratios for prior years to see if the liquidity situation has fluctuated greatly from year to year.

Other areas to look at besides the usual revenues, gross margin, operating profit, net profit and margin, and so on, are the company's short-term and, especially, long-term debt. Analyze whether the company has the means to service and pay its debt as it matures.

Reasons for Closures

Item 20 of the UFOC provides information on the franchise closures and terminations. Closures are categorized as: transfers, canceled or terminated, not renewed, re-acquired by the franchisor or a somewhat ambiguous "left the system." As a potential franchisee, you should determine the percent of closures in the system using the current year's figures. It is also helpful to calculate the percent of closures without the transfer numbers. Transfers indicate that the franchise unit has been sold by the owner. A high percentage of closures, say 10%, indicates that the franchisees may be experiencing problems. Certainly, percentages over 10% that don't count transfer numbers indicate that you might want to re-think your franchise choice.

Sometimes, a higher than average closure rate can be deceptive. There may be a reasonable explanation for a greater than usual number of franchisees leaving the system. That's why, when we are assessing a franchise opportunity at FranchiseHelp, we often call the individuals listed as closures in the UFOC. I suggest you do the same, especially if there are other troubling aspects of the franchise. So, what might you find out? Sometimes, you find out that a franchisee has left the system because she or he wishes to retire or has had a disagreement with a partner. This does not indicate anything negative about the franchise. However, at other times, you may encounter franchisees who have left the franchise because they weren't making the money they anticipated or decided to leave because of a lack of support from the franchisor. All of these revelations will help you make a decision.

Tip

Try to find out if the company-owned stores are voluntarily owned or reacquired units from struggling franchisees. Franchisors often try to hide the number of failed units by buying them back for use as company stores. Ask if they're for sale, and if they're not, you'll know that they are legitimate, company-owned stores.

FRANCHISOR'S PLAN FOR THE NEXT FIVE YEARS

When meeting with the franchise principals, you should ask them what their plans are for the next five years. First of all, you want to be sure they have a well-thought-out, comprehensive, long-term strategy and are not operating by the seat of their pants. It is also important to you as a franchisee to know the franchisor's plans for expansion, whether it plans to operate internationally, or whether it plans to add new products or services. All this can impact your business. Find out if the franchisor is keeping up with changes in the industry. You may want to ask if a research and development (R&D) department or its informal equivalent exists in the company.

Trap

Pay close attention to the franchisor's plan for growth. Beware of a franchise system that grows at an unmanageable rate. When a franchisor becomes more concerned with its growth rate than with the management of the system as a whole, not only does it lose contact with the marketplace, but the franchisees also suffer from lack of support. It's far better for you to choose a franchise that plans to grow at a manageable rate, making sure quality and control of the system never suffer.

AFTER YOU BUY THE BUSINESS—WHAT THE UFOC DOESN'T TELL YOU

When we asked a variety of franchisees in all parts of the United States what the major problems were in the first year of business, we naturally got a multitude of answers. But as we carefully analyzed the answers, we noted the following six answers came up most often as problem areas in the first year of operating a business, starting with the most common:

1. *Sales Problems.* Franchisees were challenged most by the sales end of the business, which brings with it "the need for constant sales pitches" and "cold calls." Selling requires the ability to close, to "get someone to make a decision to buy." They talked about the aftermath where they had to handle the "rejection and anxiety

involved with making sales." Although some businesses require that more time be devoted to sales than others, *every* business will require selling of some sort. There is no escape. So, if you cannot envision yourself in sales of any kind, even in small doses, you're probably not well-suited to operating a business.

2. *Getting Good Employees.* With the unemployment rate currently hovering around 5% or less, finding, hiring and keeping good employees can be difficult. Indeed, those businesses that rely heavily on minimum-wage workers find that this is a significant problem for them. One way to reduce turnover in lower-paying jobs is to offer small increases on hourly wages for periods of employment, every three months, perhaps, or for increased productivity. It also helps if the owner establishes a personal rapport with the employees. (This goes for all employees, not just minimum-wage ones.) Perhaps the best advice, though, is: *just be realistic*, since, as one franchisee told me, "no employee is ever as committed to the business as the owner."

3. *Undercapitalization.* Securely in third place is "not having enough capital." Perhaps the build-out takes longer and costs more than expected, or maybe too much inventory is bought or no additional capital is allotted for slow payers—these are just a few of the things that can impact your capital situation. The best way to avoid this problem is to go through the suggested financial exercises in Chapter 4 with an eagle eye on the bottom-line figures. If you find there's a good possibility that your projected working capital will not get you through the first year, you essentially have two choices: you can go back to your financial sources and try to raise more capital *before* you buy the franchise, or you can choose a new franchise that allows you to do business with the capital available.

4. *Sales Shortfall.* "Not reaching the projected sales figure" is the next problem area. Assuming the projected sales figures are reasonable for the business, the franchisee must sit down and analyze

all aspects of the business and pinpoint the weak links. This is a good time to call upon the franchisor's management and analytical skills in identifying anything that could be causing sales to fall short of realistic expectations.

5. *Delayed Cash Receipts.* The fifth most-mentioned problem is "late payers." Unfortunately, delayed payment happens in almost all businesses that extend credit. You can alleviate this problem if you set up a system for payments from day one. Follow up immediately if a customer does not pay by the required date, and refuse credit terms to those deemed risky. The danger in having slow payers, of course, is that you will have difficulties meeting your own payments, such as monthly salaries, royalties and suppliers' bills. You might also evaluate whether you can convert your business from one which accepts both cash and credit to one on a purely cash basis.

6. *Time Management.* "Managing priorities and operations" is the next most-cited problem. Running a business means you must prioritize tasks. Most beginning franchisees find they have too many things to do and not enough time to do all of them. This feeling of panic usually disappears when the business grows enough so that the franchisee can hire employees to share some of the tasks. The same is true for managing the operational part of the business. Inexperience is usually the culprit here, and hard work and time should solve the problem.

PROBLEMS WITH THE SYSTEM

Setbacks do occur, and businesses don't always progress the way we'd like them to. Complaining and blaming the system usually won't help the problem, but sometimes you've done everything you can, and it looks like the problem lies with the system. Here are some steps you can take:

1. *Contact the franchise system management.* Do it both verbally and, more importantly, in writing. Pinpoint and explain the problem. For example, "we can't keep customers because the products arrive late," or "the marketing and advertising material is unusable." Give as much solid documentation of the problem as you can.

2. *Inform the franchise advisory council of your problem.* If your problem is not remedied after contacting the franchisor, send a copy of the original letter explaining your problem to the advisory council. Follow up by phone and ask if the council has a plan of action. If your system doesn't have an advisory council, maybe now is the time to organize one with the other franchisees.

3. *If the system infraction is serious, consult your attorney.* See if there is a pattern with other franchisees as well. If so, ask them to document their cases.

4. *As a very last resort, take your case to court and sue the franchise system.* This course is not recommended unless the system's transgression is so blatant that nothing but the most extreme action will have the needed effect. However, in most cases the franchisor will have deeper pockets than you and can outlast you in the prolonged period it takes to settle a case in court. Accordingly, try all other methods first.

FINAL WORDS

As with any business proposition, there are no really "sure things." Your chances of choosing a good franchise are considerably improved, however, with each new piece of relevant information you possess.

7

FINDING THE BEST SOURCES
FOR FINANCING YOUR BUSINESS

It's better to lose the friend, rather than the house.

A somewhat tongue-in-cheek response when someone at a seminar on raising money for business ventures asked about the risks of asking friends and family to invest in your business.

In most cases, piecing together the financial package is a challenging, but not impossible, task. The majority of franchisees do not receive all their funding from one source. Rather, they use a combination of sources to finance their businesses. First, they see how much they can contribute from their personal savings. Then, roughly in the order of popularity, they turn to family or other investors, franchise system financing, bank loans, government programs, a note to the previous owner in the case of a resale, lines of credit, home equity loans, limited partnerships and venture capital. A discussion of these sources, as well as a few more ideas later in this chapter, should start you off on the right track to financing your chosen business.

Before you begin to try raising the necessary capital, you need to take a realistic look at the financial burdens. No matter how great a businessperson you are, chances are slim that you can put together a financial package for a major fast-food franchise that requires an investment of $750,000 or more, if you have little or no collateral. Actually, it is doubtful that you will even get this far because the lack of collateral will show up on the franchisor's qualifying questionnaire, and the evaluation process will have already come to a halt.

FINANCIAL REQUIREMENTS SET BY FRANCHISORS

Many of the franchise systems have minimum financial requirements which may, or may not, be communicated in a public way. Some systems will talk to prospective franchisees about financial stipulations only after they have reviewed the prospect's qualifying questionnaire.

In any case, be sure that the franchise of your choice is within the realm of your financial capabilities. *Before* you get into heated discussions with the franchisor, find out exactly what the franchisor considers to be the minimum financial requirements to license the franchise.

Some examples of franchisor requirements for franchisees follow (not all of which are financial).

- Del Taco, a fast-food restaurant system, requires franchisees to have a minimum net worth of $2,000,000 and minimum liquid assets of at least $250,000. A prospective franchisee must also develop a minimum of five locations to be granted a franchise. Franchisees are also required to have substantial quick-service restaurant operations experience.

- Valvoline Instant Oil Change, an auto aftermarket service, generally requires that individual licensees show a net worth of $200,000, exclusive of equity in her or his primary residence, with $100,000 of that $200,000 in cash, marketable securities or other liquid assets. Corporate and partnership licensees are expected to show the capacity and liquidity necessary to make the investment required, using the net worth and cash equivalent figures noted above.

❧ Checkers Drive-In Restaurants require that prospective franchisees have a minimum net worth of $500,000 and minimum liquid assets of $200,000 excluding personal residence.

CHOOSING A SOURCE OF CAPITAL

If you can finance the business entirely from your own personal funds and savings, congratulations, you can skip this section. If that is not the case, read on and engineer your plan of action.

Maybe you have a majority of the money needed, maybe a portion or maybe none at all. The shortfall—the money that you don't have to pay the franchisee fees, to cover the start-up costs and to fund daily operations—must be borrowed or raised.

Using Debt

If you borrow the money, you are using debt financing. You will probably borrow from one or a combination of the following: commercial banks, government-sponsored bank loans, franchise system loans, home equity loans and credit card loans. Then, too, if your franchise is a resale, you may be able to arrange a payment plan with the previous owner, whereby you pay a set amount each month to buy the business on installment.

Tip

Keep two points in mind, whatever the source of your debt financing. First, securing a loan takes a great deal of time, even if you have an impeccable credit history. Second, there is often a higher cost to borrow money than the interest alone. Many of the lending institutions charge points on the front-end for an approved loan. For example, a $20,000 loan can result in a front-end charge of $500 to $2,000, depending on your geographic location.

Using Equity

Although debt financing is far more prevalent for franchise investments, equity financing is another way to raise money. The primary difference between the two is that with debt financing, you will have an obligation to pay back the borrowed sum, but you will retain control of the business; in equity financing, however, you are giving up a part of the business to an investor or investors in exchange for their financing. The investors will claim some control of the business operations; they will own some of the assets; and they will share some earnings. You will not have a set debt obligation to repay as you would with a monthly loan payment to a bank, however. The investor will be taking a risk as to when and how much of the investment she or he will recoup, as well as whether there will be a return on the investment.

Family and Friends

One of the most common ways of finding equity financing is by having family and friends invest. They are often the first sources of financing that come to mind for many franchisees. After all, family and friends know your capabilities, and they want to help you succeed. As investors, they will, no doubt, want to have some input into how the business is run and be regularly apprised as to the progress of the venture. These demands are perfectly consistent with the role of equity investors.

The threat of problems and potential discord, however, looms larger when the family or friend investors are directly involved in the operation of the business. To be sure, some of these set-ups work very well, with everyone pulling for a common goal. However, it is more probable that you, as an owner-manager, will have to resolve conflicts between what is good for the franchise and what family or friends think is good for them. In general, you can anticipate more stress in a family-owned business, even if you are the largest stockholder. You will have to be tactful and patient with the family investors. When several family members invest in a business, the conflict often revolves around defining priorities—the business or the family.

Tip

If your business is financed by family or friends carefully consider how you will organize and operate the business to minimize potential problems.

Partnerships

Another financial route is to take a partner. In a partnership, you will share the equity of the business with another person. Such a relationship can develop by simply discussing your franchise opportunity with a friend or acquaintance and deciding to go into business together. The partnership may be established by oral or written agreement. However, I strongly encourage you to engage an attorney to formulate a written agreement that clearly details the partners' rights and obligations.

The most important thing to remember in any partnership arrangement is that the relationship must be based on trust and confidence. Your capital and your personal assets can be put on the line by a partner's actions. Whether your business thrives or fails will depend largely on your choice of partners.

Venture Capital

Another way to raise capital using business equity is to team up with a venture capital firm. Although some franchisees have received venture capital support, most venture capital firms would not even consider funding a single location franchise. They are generally chasing the big deal where the capital requirements are in the million dollar range, and where the business can generate a very high return on investment. If you are considering a multi-unit franchise deal, a large territory agreement or a high cost investment, such as a hotel or motel franchise, contacting venture capital firms should be at the top of your list.

Limited Partnership

Setting up a limited partnership is another way to sell equity in the business. The application of this method, though, has very limited use for franchisees. Limited partnerships are usually relegated to specific industries, most often the restaurant business and real estate developments. This type of partnership gives investors special tax advantages and the advantage of limited liability. If the business fails, limited partners can lose only their original investment, any additional capital contributions and their portion of the assets of the firm. General partners, however, have unlimited liability as in any ordinary partnership.

The general partner—the franchisee—is the person putting together the deal, usually someone who has managerial expertise and/or experience in the industry. The limited partners are simply investors who have little or nothing to say about the day-to-day operation of the business, but who ultimately expect to have their investment plus a nice return paid to them for the use of their capital.

Leasing

You might include a leasing arrangement in your financial planning. This doesn't quite fall under traditional debt or equity financing. Often leasing is part of the package called "franchisor-sponsored financing," and it entails paying a monthly fee to rent equipment, furnishings and fixtures from the franchisor. Usually, there is a buy-out amount at the end of the leasing period, where you have the option of buying the leased equipment or furnishings at a pre-arranged price.

Leasing can be a very attractive option. Although you will pay a greater net amount for the leased equipment, it eliminates the need of coming up with the full amount to purchase the equipment for start-up. Also, in many industries, the equipment will be obsolete in five or ten years, so when your leasing arrangement terminates, you can sign another lease for the newest models.

In addition to franchisor-sponsored leasing, commercial leasing companies write leases on everything from computers to copiers, machinery, fixtures and vehicles. Most leases are for the long-term, maybe ten years, and require the lessee to pay all the expenses related to maintenance, insurance and taxes during the lease's term. Leasing often requires collateral from the lessee—such as the pledging of assets and personal guarantees.

FIRST THINGS FIRST: A BASIC BUSINESS PLAN

Whether you are going to finance your business by using debt or equity, or by combining the two, the first step is to prepare a business plan. If you've done one before, you're ahead of the game. If not, I suggest you ask your accountant to help you prepare the financial parts of the business plan. You could also see if the franchisor offers assistance to prospective franchisees in putting together a business plan (and a loan proposal package). Several software packages and books on the market can take you through a viable business plan format step-by-step.

The purpose of the business plan is to tell would-be lenders and investors what the business is, why it's a sound investment, how the business will be operated, when you expect it to be profitable, and how you will pay back the loan or the investment.

Your starting point is the Uniform Franchise Offering Circular (UFOC). The UFOC is a detailed investment prospectus provided by the franchisor, containing much of the information you'll need to include in your business plan. In addition, since the fortunes of franchisor and franchisee are often intertwined, the lender or investor will want to know about the franchise system, as well as how you will conduct the business.

A Basic Business Plan Guide

As a guide, the following is a run down of the format and information most business plans will contain. (A sample business plan format appears at the end of this chapter.)

After a cover page, with your name (or company name), address, telephone number, the name of the business and the name of the individual or company to whom the plan is being submitted, you will normally include a table of contents. Then, we get to the body of the plan.

Summary. Often called an "executive summary," this is the most important part of your plan in terms of potential results. It gives lending officers, investors and potential partners their first (and perhaps only) impression of your venture. These people have many demands on their time, and you can't rely on them to sit down, put up their feet and casually read through your business proposal. Instead, your executive summary will have to hook them right from the beginning, in order to get them interested in knowing more about you and your proposed business. Otherwise, your proposal can land at the bottom of the pile without even a cursory review.

The summary (no longer than one or two pages) should describe the proposed franchise business with some detailing of the products or services that the franchise will sell. Next, write a brief overview of the industry, and, if possible, include some industry statistics and forecasts.

Follow up that overview with a profile of the franchise. Think about the characteristics that first sold you and emphasize those points in the summary. Also, include basic background information, such as the company's number of years in the business, number of franchise outlets and geographic range of operating franchises. Conclude with anything else that makes the franchisor stand out.

Finally, you must state the amount of the loan request, or the amount of investment money needed. Along with this goes the intended use of the capital requested—for example, building costs, working capital, inventory and equipment. Then, the sentence the reader is looking for: how and when you will repay the loan or the investment.

Tip

Ask several people whose opinions you respect to read the executive summary before you submit it. Ask them to flag both those things that capture interest and those that put the business in a negative light. Revise your summary accordingly.

Management. In the mind of the lender or the investor, the quality of the management team is of utmost importance. Potential lenders will carefully scrutinize management credentials, so bear in mind that because your business is a franchise, potential lenders and investors will also evaluate the quality of the management of the franchise system.

You need to point out how the chief executive officer and other key managers of your business are uniquely qualified to make the franchise a success. Back up these assertions with professional resumes. Remember that you're trying to make the reader feel confident about your abilities to operate the new business successfully.

If you are applying for a bank loan or a government-backed loan, you will need to include your personal financial statement (and that of any other person or persons listed as principal owners). You should already have this information on hand, since you probably submitted it to the franchisor as a first step in the qualifying process.

Business Description. You must choose whether your business will be operated as a sole proprietorship, a partnership or a corporation. Although a sole proprietorship is the simplest and least expensive way to operate a business, it is normally prudent to incorporate so that the company's liabilities are separate from your own.

The content will vary depending on the business formation selected. If you plan to do business as a corporation, include the names and addresses of the shareholders, directors and officers. If the business is a partnership, include the names and addresses of each partner. (The pros and cons of the various legal business forms are discussed in Chapter 8.)

Elaborating on information already in the summary, provide a description of the industry and your particular products or services. Include information such as the current dollar volume of the industry and the volume forecast for the next five years. Emphasize the market potential and the upward trend for the industry's products or services. For the most part, this information can be taken directly from the UFOC. You may also include pictures of products, retail locations or anything else to help the lender or investor better understand your business.

Marketing Plan. After you've described the business in somewhat general terms, then it's time to get into specific details. You need to walk the reader through a point-by-point plan as to how you will market and sell the product or service in your particular location or territory.

Tip

Don't confuse marketing with sales. Sales are the end result of a well-thought-out marketing plan.

Your business or service is not for everyone, so you will have to identify the characteristics of the people who will most likely buy your product or service. This is called "market segmentation." You will be dividing the mass market into smaller submarkets, each with unique buying characteristics. Choose the submarkets you intend to reach and identify their characteristics in this section.

The franchisor should be able to help with the information by providing you with basic demographic information on its customer base. Identify potential customers in terms of age, sex, income level, geographic dispersion, educational level and perhaps more explicit behavioral traits. You can integrate this information into your marketing plan, showing how your customer base has all the right characteristics.

Depending on the nature of your business, your description of the customer base can be general or highly specific. If you're opening a fast-food restaurant, you might say it's the entire neighborhood. If you're opening a business service, you might be very specific and say, for instance, that your customers are purchasing managers in industrial plants.

If you have a strictly defined area or locality in which to do business, state what it is. Describe the rationale behind the site selection and show how you will operate a successful business in this locale.

A thorough analysis of existing and potential *competition* in the defined marketplace is also in order. You'll have to do some homework here and find out what competing products and services are out there, how they're marketed and what they cost. Analyze the competition and then look at your own products or services. You must come up with at least one competitive advantage that can be used against your major competition. For example, maybe the quality of your product is superior, maybe the services you provide are unique, or perhaps your products or services cost 10% less than the competition. Don't overlook seemingly minor points, such as longer store hours or a more attractive location that can be developed into your competitive edge.

Next, describe how you will sell and promote your products or services. If the franchisor has a national advertising campaign to which you contribute, describe how these ad dollars are used and their expected impact on your business. Your local advertising and promotion plans will also be of interest to the reader. Indicate how your promotional money will be spent and for which media. Include innovative ideas that you have for reaching the greatest number of customers.

Financial Forecast. Since you are just starting out, you will have no actual financial data, so your financial analysis will be "pro forma." Pro forma means that the data is hypothetical and not actual. So the pro forma cash flow analysis will predict income and expenses in a future period, rather than actual performance in the past.

You can deluge the reader of your business plan with tons of financial materials. If you think it will help your case, go ahead and do it. However, you must include three types of financial statements: a pro forma balance sheet (also called "financial statement") beginning at start-up through the end of the second year, a two-year projected cash flow statement and a two-year projected profit and loss statement.

If you need help formulating the cash flow and the profit and loss statements, refer to Chapter 4. The third statement in your package is the balance sheet. Figure 7.1 shows a sample balance sheet. The sample balance sheet shows your company's financial condition for the period prior to opening. The second column is the financial state of the company at the end of year one. The third column is the financial state at the end of year two.

Figure 7.1 Sample Balance Sheet

Balance sheet as of:	Opening	Year One (End)	Year Two (End)
Assets			
Cash	$70,000	$7,312	$14,152
Accounts Receivable		12,000	13,200
Inventory		11,250	12,375
Equipment		25,000	25,000
(Less Accumulated Depreciation)		(5,000)	(10,000)
Net Equipment	0	20,000	15,000
Franchise Fee		25,000	25,000
(Less Accumulated Amortization)		(5,000)	(10,000)
Net Franchise Fee	0	20,000	15,000
Total Assets	$70,000	$70,562	$69,727
Liabilities & Owner's Equity			
Note Payable	$40,000	$37,204	$34,408
Owner's Capital			
Beginning Capital	30,000	30,000	33,358
Net Income		9,358	13,961
(Less Withdrawals)		(6,000)	(12,000)
Ending Capital	30,000	33,358	35,319
Total Liabilities & Owner's Capital	$70,000	$70,562	$69,727

153

Loan or Investment Request. The balance sheets, cash flow information and profit and loss statements culminate with a statement regarding your loan or investment needs. You must state this in precise terms and then tell the reader exactly how you will use these funds. In addition, you should indicate what your personal cash investment is, and you should spell out the terms you are requesting for either the loan or the investment.

Other Documentation. Depending on the nature of your business, some additional supporting documentation you may want to provide, include:

- A copy of your franchise agreement.
- A copy of your real estate lease agreement.
- A copy of a leasing agreement for equipment or furniture.
- A list of the insurance you carry.

Tip

When you complete your business plan, you will have a blueprint for your business. Besides the use of the business plan as a necessary money-raising tool, you will benefit personally from completing it. Writing a business plan forces you to think through all the various aspects of the business. You will find it useful to refer to the business plan periodically over the first hectic year or two to help you keep on track and refocus on your goals.

A Closer Look at Debt Financing

Since the majority of franchisees use debt financing, at least in part, to finance their franchise choice, let's look at the most popular avenues a little more closely.

When the first edition of this book was written in 1994, banks were still retrenching in an effort to repair their own balance sheets as a result of the excesses of the 1980s. However, a year or two later the climate for obtaining a bank loan for a franchise improved considerably due to the booming U.S. economy. Conditions were probably never better for those seeking franchise loans. Now, in early 1999, with failing economies in much of Asia and in Russia, the U.S. economy is slowing down and the securities market is unsteady.

Money for franchise loans from banks or other lending companies is currently not as plentiful. Mr. Agustin Mas, National Director of Franchise Lending at Banco Popular, confirms that "there is a tightening of money but money is still available. We will probably be a little more selective, a little more cautious." Banco Popular, with offices nationwide, lends money to franchisees in the following areas: the restaurant and food segment, automotive, retail/convenience store/gas stations, and printing/mailing/packages businesses. Mr. Mas emphasizes that the bank will be most interested in lending to franchisees of well-managed concepts. This is where all your research and hard work in choosing a good franchise system comes into play. If the franchisee chooses a franchise concept that is well-structured, it will be much easier to finance.

As far as requirements for the franchisee borrower, Banco Popular looks for someone with experience in the business, an investment in the business (typically 25%), a good credit history and an historical or projected capacity to repay. Loans are available for new stores, acquisitions, remodeling/re-imaging, equipment, leaseholds, real estate and refinancing.

In all cases, commercial banks are looking for an adequate amount of collateral to cover any loan they extend to you. However, the bank is not really interested in owning your house, your boat or your business real estate. The bank is looking for a certainty that you will repay the debt in full. And so, even with a pledge of your house and your own savings invested in the business, the bank may still turn you down.

Tip

Some business investments fare better with banks than others. If your business has hard assets—things like equipment, inventory and real estate—which can be used as collateral, you will have a much better chance at bank funding than a service business with only accounts receivable to offer.

The fact that your business is a franchise will help you attain a loan, since most bankers are aware of the high success statistics for franchises. But this usually isn't enough to win a "yes." You may have to think up a special angle to win the banker's confidence, especially if this is your first business. Here's how one enterprising new franchisee did it.

A Computertots (computer education for children) franchisee, Ann Brown, had relatively modest financial needs, since her franchise would be operated out of her home. She managed to cover half the investment with a loan from a relative and the other half from a bank. She prepared a business plan but backed it up with some clever market research. She called all the day care centers in her area and obtained tentative agreements from many of them to sign on with her computer program. She was able to report all this to the bank, and they were impressed. Another plus for the bank was the fact that she was already working for another franchisee, so they felt she knew the business.

Tip

If you don't have enough confidence in the probable success of the franchise to pledge your own collateral, you should re-evaluate the franchise opportunity.

SBA Loan Guarantee Programs

After being rejected by several bank for a loan, most franchisees start thinking about securing a U.S. government Small Business Administration

(SBA) loan. Unfortunately, the popular SBA loan guarantee program has a limited budget and is prone to run out of money. Demand from small businesses for the government-guaranteed loans has been growing while the budget has not. The demand for the guarantees is likely to continue to outstrip the supply. In spite of this, the International Franchise Association reported that the SBA approved loans for more than $978.5 million for franchises in 1996. Give this funding a try, but don't rely on it and certainly give yourself a back-up position.

Two Popular SBA Programs

The 7(A) Guaranteed Business Loan Program, the SBA's primary loan program, has proven to be very popular with the franchise community. The SBA set a record in 1997 by guaranteeing $8.2 billion in 7(A) loans to the small business borrower. Both fixed and variable interest rates are available. Rates are pegged at no more that 2.25% over the lowest prime rate for loans with maturities of less than seven years and up to 2.75% for seven years or longer. Rates are slightly higher for loans under $50,000.

An offshoot of the 7(A) loan program is the Low Documentation Loan Program, known as LOWDOC. Introduced in February of 1994, it is designed to streamline the SBA loan process. Loans are for $100,000 or less, and the applicant submits a one-page application form. The applicant will usually receive a response within three days.

Directives for Application

Here's how the SBA-guaranteed loan programs works. You still apply for a commercial bank loan. If the bank rejects your application for a loan on the basis of your financial profile, you become eligible to apply for an SBA-guaranteed loan. The bank you applied to may be part of the SBA-backed loan programs and, if so, will encourage you to reapply through this program. Otherwise, once a bank has rejected your loan request, you may initiate contact with the SBA yourself.

About 500 lenders, both commercial banks and non-bank lenders, participate in the SBA certification program. However, a lender does not have to be part of the certification program for you to submit an application. It could take more time to complete the process though, since the SBA gives special status to certified lenders. In addition, the SBA loan application is quite lengthy and could present a problem to someone unfamiliar with this type of document. An experienced SBA lender will often help with the paperwork or do it entirely, for a fee.

If you qualify for the SBA loan guarantee program, the government guarantees the loan for up to 90% of the value (current average is about 81%). Your loan application still goes to the lender (the bank) for initial review, and it, in turn, forwards the application and the credit analysis to the nearest SBA office. The program requires that the borrower pledge some form of collateral. If the SBA approves, the lender closes the loan and disburses the funds.

The SBA program provides a good opportunity for the lender and the borrower alike. The banks are relieved, since a larger percentage of the loan is guaranteed by the government, thereby reducing their risk. The borrower (you, the franchisee) can get long repayment periods, often not otherwise available to small businesses, at a very favorable interest rate.

In a limited number of instances, the SBA will make a direct loan (not a guaranteed loan). Availability is restricted to franchisees in high unemployment areas who are unable to obtain guaranteed loans and to disabled persons, Vietnam veterans and disabled veterans. The number of these congressionally-funded direct loans is even more limited than the SBA-guaranteed loans.

The bank you deal with for an SBA loan will do the same due diligence that it does for any commercial loan. SBA loan rejections are estimated to be 10–20% of the total. Here are some of the most common reasons for rejection:

- Franchisor does not have a registered Uniform Franchise Offering Circular. The franchisor must be registered to do business and be in good standing with the state in which the loan is applied for.

- Franchisee has past character or financial troubles. A convicted felon will rarely be granted an SBA loan. Delinquent payment histories, bankruptcies and tax liens are also viewed negatively.

- Franchisee does not have enough start-up capital. Lenders want to see around 25% of the needed amount to be provided by the borrower.

- Franchisee has submitted an unrealistic or incomplete business plan. The business plan should have a site specific marketing plan and revenue projections that are not inflated.

- The franchisor has too much control over the franchisee's operation. The SBA's charter is to assist U.S. small businesses, so accordingly, the SBA must review the franchise agreement to make sure that the amount of control over day-to-day business is not so excessive that it is actually the franchisor who controls the franchisee's operation. The SBA would then be assisting the franchisor, not the franchisee.

SBA Central Registry

The SBA Registry went online in the summer of 1998. The Registry lists the names of franchise companies that have been approved by the SBA. As mentioned above, the SBA must assess the balance of power between the franchisor and franchisee, so that the loan can indeed be qualified as aiding a small business. Historically, a review of the franchisor's contracts often took a great deal of time to complete and, since any one of the SBA's 69 local offices might perform the review, there could be inconsistent decisions. Now a franchisor can submit a worksheet and an application to the SBA contractor, Frandata Corporation, a Washington, DC, firm hired to develop and oversee the system.

If the franchise system is approved, no additional local review is required. A prospective franchisee of an approved system may then provide the SBA lender with a certification from the franchisor that there have been no subsequent revisions to the agreement. If your chosen franchise has already been approved in the Registry, the financial assistance process should be greatly sped up.

Tip

Qualifying for an SBA loan guarantee does not eliminate the need to put up your own personal collateral. The same assurances to the lender are still required, regardless of the government guarantee.

Other SBA-Related Loan Sources

The *Small Business Investment Companies (SBICs)* are independent venture capital groups licensed by the government to lend funds to small business start-ups. SBICs have access to SBA-guaranteed funds. Like most venture capital groups, SBICs often want an equity stake in the company and a managerial role. There is generally long-term loan financing in exchange for the equity position.

You'll find SBICs in most cities in the United States, some of which are bank affiliates or subsidiaries of other financial institutions. Some of the SBICs even specialize in working with franchisees. For a list of SBICs, call or write to the National Association of Small Business Investment Companies, 512 Washington Bldg., Washington, DC, 20005, (202) 638-3411.

SYSTEM FINANCING AND LEASING

About 30% of the franchise systems in the U.S. have a program in place that aids the franchisee in financing the business and/or leasing the necessary facilities and equipment. Franchisors offer this service to make their franchises more attractive. Also, offering financing allows the franchisor to sign up people who fit their ideal franchisee criteria, but are deficient in financial capabilities. Here are some of the types of programs available:

  ❧ The Cendant Corporation is the parent company for Travelodge, a full-service hotel facility, and the franchisor of Travelodge Hotels, Inc. The company may defer the initial fee for a fixed period, usually 90 days, if circumstances warrant. If five or more hotels are franchised, each having 100 or more rooms, Travelodge, or a Cendant financial company, may lend the franchisee a Development Advance loan. Alternately, the franchisee may receive temporary royalty benefits in the form of rate reductions, credits or rebates if certain criteria are met.

  Cendant has also implemented a special financing program for qualified African-American and Hispanic franchisees. The financing provides the franchisee a Development Advance of up to $1,000 per guest room for facilities up to 75 rooms and $1,500 per guest room for those with over 75 guest rooms.

  ❧ The Southland Corporation, franchisor of 7-Eleven stores, offers financing for all or a portion of the franchise fee or down payment in limited situations where a qualified applicant displays a financial hardship that makes it difficult for the applicant to pay all the initial fees. In this case, the fee must be repaid in up to 60 monthly installments, beginning with the first month that the franchisee takes possession of the store.

  Southland also offers financing for the entire franchise fee in the Work-To-Own Program. The Program enables 7-Eleven employees who successfully manage corporate stores located in Michigan, Illinois, Indiana, Ohio and Missouri to apply for a franchise and, if qualified, to receive certain benefits. For example, 7-Eleven will finance the entire franchise fee for the store for up to five years, pursuant to a promissory note, if a manager qualifies.

Sometimes the franchisor provides the financing, and other times the franchisor enlists a third party to provide the help. In the last few years, a number of franchise finance companies have emerged and large, prestigious investment and financial firms have set up divisions to originate franchise loans. A number of these lenders also put together pools of loans, which are then securitized to be sold in the bond market. The advent of franchise loan securitization has been most beneficial to multi-unit franchisees, who are already successful in their businesses, providing them with access to low-cost capital. Most of these loans have been made to franchisees in the restaurant industry.

One of the third party financing companies is GreenTree Franchise Finance, a Conseco Company. Mark Luke, Vice President, National Credit Manager, says that "gaining finance for a first unit franchise from a company such as GreenTree is still difficult. The SBA is probably a much better route for an initial unit." GreenTree, for example, is most interested in financing a franchisee with a minimum of five units, an owner that has a minimum of three years in the business and a franchise which is a Tier 1 or two concept. Major industries for GreenTree, and other similar financial companies, are food concepts (quick-service restaurants [QSR] and casual dining), auto aftermarket concepts, hotels and convenience stores/gas stations.

Talk to some of the larger finance companies and you'll hear franchise systems being referred to as "Tier 1," "Tier 2," etc. (as above in the Green-Tree evaluation of a system). If your goal is to become a multi-unit or area developer franchisee, the informal grading of a franchisee system by lenders is something you should know about.

The grading is, for the present, most applicable to restaurant systems. It is unofficial and there is certainly disagreement among financing companies about which concept merits which tier.

In brief, a Tier 1 concept is a national brand with 1000+ units. It is a publicly traded company and holds investment grade bond ratings. Franchises like Wendy's and Burger King are included here.

A Tier 2 concept would have a minimum of five years of franchising, good profit and growth numbers and a rapid growth in franchise units.

Tier 3 concepts are regional, but dominant in the areas where they compete, and have steady, historic streams of cash flow.

Tier 4 concepts are question marks. If loans are offered to the franchisees of these concepts, the lender bets that the concept will survive at least the term of the loan.

Equipment Leasing

Since equipment often comprises 25–75% of the start-up costs, leasing the equipment can be a very effective way to cut down on your up-front cash needs. Leasing can be handled directly by the franchisor or by a leasing firm.

Franchisors with heavy equipment needs such as restaurants, lawn services and hair salons often make arrangements with leasing firms if they are unable to offer their own leasing programs.

The franchisee will usually pay a rate about 2–3% higher than commercial banks when using these companies. However, since small business loans through commercial banks are often difficult to obtain, the higher interest rate can be an acceptable trade-off. Also, unlike traditional lenders' requirements for personal equity or collateral, the leasing firm uses the leased asset as collateral. The leasing firms often have a close relationship with the franchisor and sometimes require the franchisor to sign a repurchase agreement as additional security against default.

HOMES AND CREDIT CARDS

There's no doubt that many franchisees rely on home equity loans or second mortgages to finance their new businesses. If you don't own your home or don't have sufficient equity in it, this option is not open to you. If putting your home on the line as collateral makes you very nervous, however, I would investigate all other options first.

Tip

Stuart Ruben, a Money Mailer franchisee, recommends "using a home equity line of credit that you can draw on. But get the line before you buy the franchise—when you have an income coming in."

Several franchisees we interviewed used lines of credit from credit card companies. Although no disasters were reported, this should be a last resort type of financing, since the interest rates are normally very high and you can be seduced into paying only minimal monthly amounts when cash flow is tight. In general, if you must use these credit lines, look for the lowest interest rates and draw on the lines only for small sums that you expect to repay quickly.

SPECIAL FINANCING PROGRAMS FOR SPECIFIC GROUPS

In the past, women, minorities and veterans were frequently at a disadvantage when it came to buying a business. Often, they were qualified in one respect but lacked another element—collateral, net worth or business experience—that traditional financial institutions require. Now franchising systems are welcoming these groups into the franchisee fold. Some franchise systems are leveling the playing field by providing special management and financial programs for these candidates. These new incentives, coupled with federal, state and local government programs, make investing in a franchise a real possibility for a more diverse group of people.

Nearly one of every four Americans is a member of the African-American, Hispanic, Native American or Asian communities. Some franchisors are responding to these numbers by setting up formal minority franchise recruitment programs. Others are at least showing increased sensitivity to the special needs of minority franchisees.

Some of the most impressive programs for minorities have been instituted at the larger fast-food franchisors. The minority programs in place at KFC (Tricon Global Restaurants, Inc.) and Hardee's are two good examples.

Although the franchise system itself is probably the most effective force for minority involvement, the federal government is also working to bring diverse groups into franchising. The U.S. Department of Commerce's Minority Business Development Agency has a nationwide network of centers set up to counsel minority individuals.

State and local programs are one of the very best places to look for managerial and financial help. Most states have a division of business development specifically geared toward minority and women's needs. Also, many states are showing a keen interest in franchise businesses as a way to promote commercial growth in the state.

Maryland's state program is routinely praised for its excellence. The state pioneered a franchise financing assistance program designed specifically for minorities, which includes ethnic minorities, women and disabled individuals. This program, the Maryland Equity Participation Investment Program (EPIP), approved by the state legislature in 1985, established an equity fund to assist in minority purchases of franchises. EPIP is administered through the Maryland Small Business Development Financing Authority (MSBDFA).

Pennsylvania also has a program that aids minorities in their franchise choices. Through the Pennsylvania Minority Business Development Authority's Franchise Finance and Technical Assistance Program, the state offers long-term, low-interest loans of up to $750,000 to individuals investing $5,000 to $50,000. Besides financial help, consultants provide free analysis of franchise opportunities for the applicant.

In New York, franchise loans are also available through the New York State Minority and Women Revolving Loan Fund of the Urban Development Corporation. As the title implies, both ethnic minorities and women may use this source. The amount of the loans ranges from $20,000–$200,000, or twice the amount of the cash investment of the franchisee, whichever is less. Generally a minimum of 10% cash equity must be invested by the business owner. In addition, to qualify, the franchise system must be nationally known (with operations in at least three states and at least 15 franchise locations). Preference is given to franchises that are located in distressed areas.

If you are not based in Maryland, Pennsylvania or New York, contact the Office of Minority and Small Business Development in your state capitol. Virtually all the states, although with varying degrees of expertise, have some sort of program in place that will assist the minority small business owner.

Tip

Have you ever noticed that you usually get better results—especially when dealing with a bureaucratic agency—if you do it in person? *Whenever possible, try to set up a meeting with the key decision maker.*

FINAL WORDS

If you are convinced (assuming you've done everything we talked about in the preceding chapters) that your choice will result in a profitable business, go ahead and look at all these sources of financing. Combine two, three or more sources in any way that makes sense for you.

Figure 7.2 Business Plan Guide

Cover Page
Name (your name or company name):_____
Address:_____
_____
Telephone: (_____)_____
Name of Business:_____
Business Plan Submitted to:_____

Table of Contents
Summary   Page____
Management   Page____
Business Description   Page____
Marketing Plan   Page____
Financial Forecast   Page____
Loan (or Investment) Request   Page____
Other Documentation   Page____

Summary
Brief statements of following: business description (products or services), overview of industry, franchise profile, amount of loan request or investment capital needed, intended use of the capital and details on repayment of loan or investment capital.

Management
Names, addresses, ages, education and business experience of CEO and other key personnel.

Personal financial statement of prospective franchisee and any other principal owners if applying for a bank or government backed loan.

Names and experience of franchisor's top management.

Business Description
Legal business form (sole proprietorship, partnership or a corporation).

For sole proprietorship: name and address of owner. For partnership: names and addresses of each partner. For corporation: names and addresses of the shareholders, directors and officers.

General information on industry and franchise.

Marketing Plan
Customer base (demographics).
Rationale for site selection.
Analysis of the competition.
Advertising and promotional plans.

Financial Forecast
Pro forma balance sheet.
Projected cash flow.
Projected profit and loss.

Loan or Investment Request
State the amount of your loan or investment needs, use of the funds and the terms you are requesting.

Other Documentation
Anything else that will help your case or help the reader better understand the business.

8
UP AND RUNNING

My advice is to follow the system. That really makes you successful, especially in the first few years. Many of the franchises not doing well don't follow the system.
   LISA BRUMM
   Formals Etc. (rental formalwear) franchisee

A better title for this chapter might be "Up and Running—Almost." Once you've chosen the franchise, signed the agreement, set up the financing and gone through training, you still have to:

- ❧ Choose the legal business form.
- ❧ Negotiate real estate leases and rents.
- ❧ Buy equipment and inventory.
- ❧ Supervise structural changes and the "build-out."
- ❧ Recruit and select employees.
- ❧ Plan local promotions and advertising.

Each of these phases can have an impact on the success of your start-up. This chapter will take you through the basic steps involved and share a tip or two from some franchisees who have been there. In addition, you'll get some advice on what to do when the ownership of the franchise system changes and how to react to a franchisor's financial problem—including bankruptcy. Lastly, you'll want to know what's involved in selling your business—hopefully, only after many years of great success.

CHOOSING THE BUSINESS STRUCTURE

You will have to choose among three basic business structures before you open your doors for business: the sole proprietorship, the partnership and the corporation. Because each differs in its setup cost, tax consequences and legal liability, I strongly advise you to consult with both an attorney and an accountant before making your decision. (See also Figure 8.1 at the end of this chapter for a comparative chart of various business structures.)

Sole Proprietorship

The sole proprietorship is simple and easy to organize. All you'll have to do is apply for a federal ID number and, in many states, obtain a state and/ or municipal sales tax number. The expenses of starting a sole proprietorship are minimal because there is little legal documentation.

The sole proprietor owns all the stock in the business and keeps all the profits. However, the owner will also have to come up with all the capital to start and operate the business. Making decisions is easy; you don't have to consult with anyone else unless you want to. This is a distinct advantage when a quick response to an opportunity is a necessity. The sole proprietor doesn't have to file a separate business income tax form. All the franchise income, expense, profit and loss are transferred to the owner's personal tax return.

The biggest disadvantage of the sole proprietorship is the personal liability incurred from business operations. This structure offers no shelter from the claims of creditors. A successful lawsuit against a sole proprietor's business can result in a lien on the personal assets of the owner. Another disadvantage is that sole proprietorship makes no provision for the continuation of the business after the owner's death or retirement. There is no true continuity of management and ownership title.

Partnership

To qualify as a partnership, the franchise has to be owned by two or more persons who have a financial interest in the business. A partnership is easy to set up. In fact, it only requires two or more people agreeing to go into business together and doesn't even require a formal agreement—although a formal written agreement drawn up by an attorney is strongly advised.

A partnership, like a sole proprietorship, doesn't file a business tax return, but it is required to file an information return (Form 1065) signed by one of the partners. This form reports gross income, deductions and the names of the owners with proportionate ownership. Each partner is liable for her or his commensurate share of the taxes resulting from the business. Unless a partnership agreement stipulates otherwise, profits and losses must be divided among partners according to their ownership ratio. Partners are personally responsible for the debts of the partnership, and the partnership will not shelter the participants from the personal liability of creditors' demands.

A partnership agreement should explicitly state the provisions for adjusting to the death or termination of a partner; otherwise, the partnership is legally dissolved. The amount and method of payment for a partner's interest upon her or his termination or death should be clearly specified in the agreement. Without this stipulation, a long and bitter confrontation is the usual outcome if the partnership is dissolved.

Tip

Choosing a partnership structure for your franchise business can be a hazardous decision. The most frightening aspect is the fact that you are not just responsible for your actions, as in a sole proprietorship, but you can also be held liable for the actions of any of your partners. Unlike a corporation, your personal assets can be confiscated for business judgments.

Corporation

A corporation is a group of individuals who are legally treated as a single person. It is a separate and distinct entity from that of its owners or stock-holders. It is more costly and more time-consuming to set up than a sole proprietorship or a partnership. For example, a fee is payable at the time the charter or articles of incorporation are filed with the state agency. Additional costs include attorney's fees and other charges, such as stock certificates and a corporate seal. You must get a federal ID number for use on federal tax returns and other documents. Also, you'll have to comply with state and local requirements for business licenses. The record keeping and reporting for the corporation will be more complex than for a sole proprietorship or a partnership. You will probably also find that the required reports cause some loss of privacy and confidentiality.

The biggest plus for choosing a corporate structure is the limited liability. Personal liability is limited to the amount of money used to buy stock in the company, unlike the sole proprietorship and partnership, which put the participant's entire net worth at risk for creditor satisfaction. Investors in a corporation avoid this total exposure. It's important to consult your attorney about fulfillment of your corporate responsibilities so that no one can "pierce the corporate veil" (the protection the corporate structure affords your personal assets is referred to as the "corporate veil"). Corporate responsibilities vary from state to state.

The corporation is unaffected by death or termination of a stockholder. However, the transfer or inheritance of stock can affect the ownership and control of the corporation. A corporation pays taxes much like an individual. It will file a tax return and will pay taxes on profits. The stockholders, in turn, will pay personal taxes on salaries and dividends.

There is a special entity called an "S corporation" that combines several of the advantages of both a partnership and a corporation. It is taxed like a partnership with gains and losses passed through to individual stockholders, but without the personal liability that is associated with a partnership. However, the disadvantage is that loss deductions for tax purposes can't exceed the amount a shareholder has invested in the business. For example, if you invest $100,000 in a corporation, that is the maximum amount you can deduct from your taxes as a loss. With the partnership format, however, you could invest the same amount ($100,000), but deduct $150,000 or more, if that is your share of the losses. In addition, a Chapter S corporation is restricted to certain kinds of businesses and can't have more than 35 stockholders.

Tip

It often pays to operate a business as an S corporation in the beginning years so that losses can be passed through to the shareholders for tax purposes. When the business becomes profitable, you can terminate the S status and elect the regular C corporate status.

Tip

Be very careful with timing if you want to elect S status or you will lose out. To be eligible, a new corporation must file for election in the 75-day period after the corporation has begun its first tax year. The beginning is defined when the corporation issues stock to stockholders, acquires assets or begins to do business—whichever occurs first.

HOW TO NEGOTIATE WITH THE "BARRACUDAS"

Once you have chosen a business structure, you can go on to decisions that relate to the operation of the franchise. If you're operating a retail business, you probably have already settled on the location. One of the more difficult tasks still has to be tackled—negotiating a lease with a mall developer or landlord.

One franchisee said to me, "Mall developers are barracudas. You must learn to deal with them. It's very cutthroat." That certainly has not been the experience of every franchisee. You might be lucky enough to negotiate with very honest, cooperative and accommodating landlords. But since being prepared is half the battle, here is some information and some suggestions to better prepare you for the negotiations.

Tip

Signing a lease entails rights and obligations, so let your attorney review it before you sign anything. It's also a good idea to take along an expert from franchise management to help you with lease negotiations. Lastly, consult your insurance agent to look into the possibility of renter liability if you are leasing a space or a building.

All leases contain basic provisions such as rental amount, term of lease, commencement date, description of the premises and renewal options. Beyond this, leases cover the specific needs and requirements of the landlord. It is in your best interest for you—along with your attorney—to read the lease carefully and negotiate those provisions that pose a problem.

Don't try to rush through the negotiations. They might not be easy or fun, but taking the time to make sure it's the best agreement for your business is worthwhile. Often franchisees quickly sign a lease only to find themselves in a no-profit situation or even facing a business failure. Lisa Brumm, a Formals Etc. franchisee, has this advice for all potential lease signers: "If you want a location badly and you let it show, you won't be able to negotiate. You must be able to walk away from the table. It may be the perfect mall or office building, but most likely there are other good ones out there."

Tip

Wee-Bag-It franchisee Marcy Pinnell, with the expert help of the franchisor, was able to negotiate an "18-month kick-out clause" with the landlord. The clause stipulated that if her business was not profitable within 18 months, she could give up the five-year lease and pay three or four months' rent in a lump sum as settlement in full to the landlord. Try this—with the franchisor's assistance.

Aside from questioning the costs and benefits of the existing lease clauses, pay attention to the following:

1. *Coordinate the term of the real estate lease with the term of the franchise agreement.* For example, if your franchise agreement is for five years, try to sign the lease for five years.

2. *Ask the landlord to write in lease renewal options.*

3. *Note the date that rent commences.* If possible, try not to pay any rent before the premises are ready for occupancy. For example, you do not want to pay rent while the space is getting painted or the equipment and fixtures are getting installed.

4. *Ask for a few months of free rent in return for signing a long-term lease.*

5. *Be sure there is a clause allowing you the right to assign or sublet the premises in case you decide to sell the franchise.*

6. *Negotiate hard to pay a fixed rent rather than a percentage rent.* Percentage rents usually work like this: the franchisee pays a minimum rent until her or his business hits a target gross sales figure, at which point a higher rent based on a percentage of gross sales kicks in.

Tip

If you absolutely can't escape a percentage rent clause (shopping center management can be adamant about this), put your efforts into negotiating the very highest gross sales escalation point you can. For example, push for the percentage rent to kick in at $300,000 rather than $200,000.

7. *Ask for exclusivity clauses that prevent competing businesses from operating in the same location.*

8. *Negotiate with the landlord to participate in the cost of signage and structural work.*

In some cases, you may find that arranging a lease entails dealing with the franchisor, not the mall developer or landlord. Some franchisees pay rent to the franchisors, who hold the leases. Often the rent is paid monthly, calculated on the basis of gross sales. This, too, is a percentage rent, so be careful. In another scenario, the franchisor builds the premises for the franchisee and then leases it back to the franchisee. Alternatively, the franchisor may build and then sell the premises to a sale-and-leaseback company who will then become the franchisee's landlord.

Trap

If the landlord and the franchisor are one and the same, don't assume it has your best interests at heart. Negotiate these leases as carefully as you would with any landlord.

INSTALLING THE INNER WORKINGS

After you've settled rents and leases to your satisfaction, you'll have some decisions to make about store design, equipment and inventory. The franchisors often set certain specifications and limits. To meet these guidelines and to accommodate your personal business needs, you might want to make some structural changes in the leased space before opening.

Tip

Be sure the space is suitable for your business. One franchisee explained how a food product had to be made fresh daily, but the space did not lend itself to efficient production. If it takes 25% more time, for example, to perform a task or to produce a product because the space is not appropriate, your bottom line will certainly suffer.

The time it takes to select and install the most suitable equipment and furniture will correspond indirectly with the age and sophistication of the system you're buying into. The older, larger franchise systems usually have the outfitting of the premises down to a science. Everything should be mapped out for you in terms of the best equipment, where to place it and how to install it. In contrast, one of the newer systems or a start-up franchise will not have such tried and true suggestions. Ken Wisotzky remembers that when he opened his My Favorite Muffin franchise, the franchisor didn't help with the placement and installation of the baking equipment. He was pretty much on his own and had to work out logistical problems by trial and error.

Even with some large, well-seasoned franchise systems, franchisees frequently encounter problems. For example, two franchisees of the same large fast-food system had complaints about the start-up.

One franchisee found that "overall, the coordination of the equipment set-up was lacking." The franchisee bought most of the necessary equipment—costing almost $250,000—from the franchisor because the prices were competitive. But, he goes on to say, "The right hand didn't know what the left hand was doing. We had mistakes with the walk-in freezers and, also, we found out that some items we purchased we could have done without and other equipment we needed, we were never advised to buy. It was a very costly error."

The second franchisee in this large system complained that the franchisor was not always organized and made mistakes because they did not communicate with franchisees. He illustrated this confusion by describing the decision of buying uniforms for employees. The franchisor sent him a book of uniforms with six styles to choose from. The franchisee thought there should be one standard uniform. In any case, he read further and found out that four of the styles would be discontinued the next year. Of course, these styles were the ones that appealed to him. He bemoaned the fact that he didn't know how many uniforms to order and that if he ordered the wrong sizes or not enough, he could not re-order because they would be discontinued.

Tip

"Don't invest in showy offices, taking clients to lunch and Christmas gifts," says Larry Gambino, Priority Management franchisee, "it's more important to give good customer service."

Tip

Jim Gendreau, a Cost Cutters multiple-unit franchisee, says, "Be conservative in your office. For example, my corporate office is furnished with cheap furniture. Why? I only invest in things that make money. Furniture doesn't make money."

Calculating inventory requirements can also be a trial-and-error process. Ken Wisotzky had two sets of inventory problems with his side-by-side franchises in a retail shopping mall. In the Gloria Jean's coffee store, he found that he bought too much inventory because he opened the store during its slowest month. Based on that experience, he advises others to study the sales figures or to talk to other franchisees to find out the patterns and to adjust your opening inventory accordingly.

Meanwhile, in Wisotzky's My Favorite Muffin franchise, the inventory problem was even more complex. With muffins—or any food product made fresh daily—you have to guess at the quantity, and in this case, the flavors. Wisotzky says, "[In the beginning] there was a lot of waste because we weren't too sure what and how much our clientele would buy. But now [after over four years] there's almost no waste."

In other instances, inventory decisions can involve staffing problems as well. For example, Florence and George Hayden, in operating their Wendy's franchise, had to decide not only how much fresh food to prepare, but how much time they would need to prepare it. After a few days of operation, they realized they had to have the staff in their restaurant start at 7 a.m. for a 10:30 to 11 a.m. opening. Chili, for example, takes four hours to cook (they figured out later that it could be cooked the night before), and slicing onions, lettuce and other vegetables for the salad bar took a few hours, even with four to six people working.

Tip

Time the opening of your business carefully. Many franchisees advise against opening the business at the busiest time of year. First impressions can be lasting impressions. You may not have a second chance with customers if they encounter poor or inefficient service or an untrained staff.

MANAGING THE "BUILD-OUT"

When talking about construction and structural changes, called the "build-out," we often hear words like "horrible" and "nightmarish." Those reactions were the result of snafus such as:

- The franchisor's estimated set-up costs are based on the costs of goods, services and labor in a cheaper region. Be aware of wide variations in pricing for different parts of the country.

- Unanticipated local and government regulations can add charges or changes for the franchisee.

- Unethical or poorly managed construction crews who do a poor job can dramatically inflate the costs.

Most franchise systems adjust their estimates to reflect the fact that construction costs are higher in some areas, especially in the New York City metropolitan area and in certain areas of California. Union labor costs are often one of the reasons for disparate costs in the country. Even so, if you are in a part of the country where costs are traditionally higher, take the franchisor's high-end estimate and add 10% to arrive at your probable build-out costs.

Trap

Jeff Grayson, a multi-unit Pizzeria Uno franchisee, found his franchisor's estimated costs were too low because it did "not calculate sales tax and installation charges for equipment in the initial costs." In Grayson's case, this added an additional 15% to the estimated cost and, at times, could add as much as 20%.

Another thing to do before beginning work on the build-out is to look into municipal codes. Leslie Goldberg and her partner Mark Weintraub opened their Expressions Custom Furniture franchise in a new strip center in a completely empty building. Consequently, they had to construct walls, put in electrical wiring and take care of other basics. Conforming to the numerous building codes and regulations covering light construction added extra time and extra costs to the construction.

Government regulations can also be a source of added expense. During the construction of the Hayden's second Wendy's restaurant, an inspector from a federal government agency visited the construction site and informed them that there was improper access for disabled persons. To comply with the regulation stipulation that disabled persons should not have to cross any traffic to gain entrance to a business, the Hayden's had to stop construction and revise their plans.

Hiring the wrong people to work on your build-out can be the biggest nightmare of all. In some areas of the country, construction people are bonded and don't get paid until the work is satisfactorily finished. This was not the case when a husband and wife franchisee did extensive construction on a store in the Northeast. They found themselves enmeshed in a tough lawsuit because, although they paid the general contractor, he didn't pay the sub-contractors. The sub-contractors, in turn, demanded payment from the franchisee.

You can avoid these problems by getting referrals on all the general construction people before you hire them. Then, don't do anything structurally until you talk to the architect, the plumber, the electrician and the carpenter, to be sure all of them know what they are doing. Go over the plans with each worker to be certain the plans make sense. Then, firm up all the costs and get them in writing. You may have to pay some up-front money for materials, but don't pay the entire agreed upon sum until everything is done to your satisfaction.

Tip

A restaurant owner gave us this advice. "Try to find a failed restaurant site. You can save a lot of money by using old restaurant premises. For example, the air conditioning, all the services from the street, much of the kitchen equipment, toilets, sewage and so on are there. Restaurant owners can save 30–40 % by going into a shell. That frees up more cash for the front of the store instead of sinking it into buried sewer pipes and the like." Here's another way to save money: If the kitchen equipment has not been installed and is not prescribed or leased by the franchisor, try to buy it at an auction. You may end up paying as little as 25% of the standard price for slightly used equipment.

EMPLOYEES: THE HEART OF THE BUSINESS

Ideally, you're going to hire people who are not only good workers— capable, energetic, conscientious—but also people you like. If you spend 40–60 hours a week together, it really helps if you like each other.

Every business has a slightly different twist on selecting, hiring and retaining employees, but, in general, most employee-related problems revolve around high turnover rates, motivating employees, training them and finding ones with specialized skills.

Franchisees are always looking for ways to bring out the best in their low wage employees. One restaurant franchisee we talked to was testing a program where, for example, if an employee knew all the items on a menu, she or he would get a $.25 raise. In addition, raises could be given for competencies in other areas.

One franchisor, Round Table Pizza, according to one of its franchisees, has an innovative program to help their franchisees deal with employees.

The system operates a hotline for the franchisee called "Shift Fill." If an employee is sick or extra help is needed, the franchisor will attempt to send the needed personnel to the franchisee.

Tip

Here's a great idea to use when you start out and need sales, but have little money for employees. Fred Banty and five other Connecticut Padgett Business Services franchisees joined together to hire one salesperson to prospect for sales. The six share the cost of one salesperson.

Motivation, in part, seems to correlate with the economic situation of your region of the country. In areas where jobs are highly valued or there is a high unemployment rate, there seems to be no problem filling the ranks with motivated employees. However, with the very healthy economy of the last few years, procuring and retaining good employees has been difficult almost everywhere. The best advice is to simply create a pleasant work atmosphere where your employees know their good work will be valued. If this is not enough, you will just have to struggle through this time of low unemployment—until the next economic downturn.

Then there are some businesses in which the franchisee must spend what seems to be an inordinate amount of time dealing with employees' issues. Jeanette Fuller, a Tutor Time franchisee, says, "Dealing with employees is a major part of running a day-care center for children six weeks to five years old." Fuller considers staffing her biggest challenge. Employees find it difficult to work eight hours a day with toddlers, and so Fuller primarily hires part-timers who can keep their enthusiasm level high for the shorter time. Employees calling in "sick" is often a problem, since she must replace the person on short notice.

Tip

College campuses are a great source for good part-time employees. Call local universities for business students.

PLANNING LOCAL PROMOTIONS AND ADVERTISING

When you open a new business, you want everyone to know about it. Even better, you'd like a lot of people to try out your product or service. To that end, depending upon your choice of franchise, you may have to do a lot or a little promotion. If your franchise is part of a start-up system or one that only has a few franchises, you'll have to create an identity through a local promotional campaign that tells potential customers about the products or services you're offering. However, in the case of one of the nationally-known franchises, you'll do less on a local level because the instant name recognition will bring customers to you. In both cases, though, franchisees will do some local advertising and promotions to launch their new businesses.

Finding the best ways to advertise and promote products and services is essentially a process of trial and error. No doubt, you'll make mistakes in the beginning. You might find, like Fred Banty of Padgett Business Services, that local advertisements don't work as well as cold calls, tele-marketing, and referrals for finding customers. Leslie Goldberg, an Expressions Custom Furniture franchisee in a New York City suburban community, found that advertising can bring business, but reports that, "We spent too much money on advertising and got very little impact for it at first." She has refined her advertising placements by asking every person who walks into the furniture store where she or he heard or read about the store. In this way, she can tell which advertisements have the best draw.

Timing promotions for major impact and the best results is another challenge. Prior to opening their Wendy's franchise, Florence and George Hayden promoted the store opening heavily. They advertised extensively in local newspapers and announced free prizes at the opening. Then, they had some public relations nights. One was a "parents' night," where all the parents of the workers were invited and the employees served and practiced on them. A "VIP Night" was next where they invited the contractors, community leaders, clergy, family and friends.

In the end, all this advertising and promotion worked too well. George Hayden says, "For over four weeks, the business was so strong that the staff couldn't keep up. The kids were so tired that they called in sick after four days." (The Hayden's did win a sales prize from Wendy's for top opening week sales.) This experience leads them to advise other franchisees to open up a store without much fanfare and then, a week or so later, have a grand opening after most of the bugs have been worked out.

Tip

To make all openings go smoother, hire a key person—someone with a good deal of industry experience—to head up your staff.

POTENTIAL PROBLEMS WITH THE FRANCHISOR

Since the fate of the franchisor and franchisee is always intertwined, it's important to know how to react to a franchisor problem. Two potential scenarios, a change of corporate ownership and serious franchisor financial difficulties, are discussed with suggestions for appropriate franchisee actions.

Consequences of New Corporate Ownership

A change in franchise ownership can be good or bad for franchisees. A new owner can bring in additional resources, maybe a bigger customer base or better financing for the franchisees. Or a new owner can bring increased franchise fees or inflated prices of supplies and products in order to finance the purchase. Also, the new manage-ment might be inexperienced and execute bad decisions.

A change in management can be disruptive, particularly when the executive office has a revolving door. The owner of a business brokerage business was able to survive six changes of system ownership by "keeping

[his] focus on selling businesses," despite the chaos. In another instance, after watching the franchise owners going public and then going private several times, the franchisees formed a separate franchisee organization in self-defense. Finally, lacking confidence in the leadership of each succeeding ownership group, many of the franchisees stopped paying royalties, dropped the logo and started conducting business independently.

In another corporate changeover example, a retail snack food franchisee was successful and happy for several years with the original franchise owners. When the originators of the concept sold out to a large conglomerate, everything changed. The franchisee says, "They now had a bunch of people who knew how to spend money [franchisees, for example, were flown out to corporate headquarters to be wined and dined], but lost touch with the basics." In addition, the system turned out vast quantities of product, but the product quality declined, and the franchisees couldn't sell the huge amount of product. This meant the franchisees had to continually run specials to move the product. Eventually the conglomerate gave up on the franchise and a succession of new owners followed. Now our franchisee is giving up on the franchisor.

What can a franchisee do, if anything, to avoid the potential problem of changing ownership? Our unhappy franchisee above says, "In retrospect, I would have tried to incorporate into the franchise agreement that if the company is sold or changed, I would have the option to get out of the contract."

From a franchise attorney's viewpoint, Bret Lowell tells us, "Assume when you buy the franchise that the management will change—sometimes for the best, but sometimes for the worst." He points out that even mature companies change, and, in all companies, an evolutionary process takes hold.

From a legal standpoint, you can do little to prevent a franchise company from being sold, so look at the age and goals of the owners when you investigate the franchise. Also, find out how dedicated they are to the industry; this should give you some indication as to whether a corporate change might be imminent. But there are no guarantees, so this question of corporate changeover remains one of the areas of risk when you buy a franchise.

Effects of a Franchisor Bankruptcy

In May of 1998, my company, FranchiseHelp, completed a study that examined the effects of franchisor bankruptcies on the franchisees. We looked at a variety of recent franchisor bankruptcies and then more intensively researched three restaurant companies that had recently filed for Chapter 11 bankruptcy. Many of our findings came as a result of talking to franchisees in each of the systems. Contrary to what most corporate franchise management had been saying for years—the franchisor's problems do not impact the franchisee's businesses—we found that franchisees are indeed affected by a franchisor bankruptcy. The effects, however, can be minor, somewhat serious or very serious, even culminating in the franchisee's bankruptcy or closure. How well you fare as a franchisee depends, in a large part, on certain actions that can be taken by both you, the franchisee, and the franchisor.

First, let's look at what the franchisor can do. Too often, the franchisor likes to keep its financial problems quiet, and it is only when a public announcement or a bankruptcy filing must be made that the franchisee gets an inkling of a potentially serious situation. In a time of financial difficulty, the major action of the franchisor should be to alert the franchisee community as early as possible and keep the franchisee abreast of the current situation by frequent communications. In addition, the franchisor should consider using many and frequent press releases that emphasize the business of the system goes on and that the franchisees in the system are operating and doing business as usual.

If the franchisor does not notify the press as suggested, you as the franchisee can urge the franchisor to do so and ask other franchisees to voice their concerns to the franchisor. Large multi-unit franchises may alert the local newspapers and publications that the franchisor bankruptcy has not affected their business.

Franchisees in these situations may want to investigate the possibility of organizing a franchise committee to deal with a Chapter 11 and other financial scenarios, with the goal of best preserving both the franchisees' and franchisor's businesses. Franchisees, in general, are becoming more pro-active and several groups have formed separate franchise associations to protect the franchisee's interests at the time of a franchisor bankruptcy.

Tip

The public often falsely associates the individual franchise with that of the bankrupt franchisor. If you are in this unfortunate situation, and you begin to receive negative customer feedback about the viability of your business, do everything you can to publicize the fact that your business is alive, well and operating in spite of the franchisor's troubles.

SELLING YOUR BUSINESS

We hope you will only think about selling your business after many years of successful operation. But, sometimes personal or financial considerations make it necessary to transfer the ownership of your franchise. The ability to sell or transfer your franchised business is an important part of the franchise agreement. Check the franchise agreement to see what the franchisor's stipulations are for resales. You should also check to see that the franchise is assignable and that it may be sold if you die or are disabled.

Franchisors have an overriding interest in knowing who will be buying your business, because they will expect the sales level to be maintained and they will want to know that the owner can pay the royalties and other fees. In most cases, franchisees must ask the franchisor for approval of a transfer. In practice, most resales that make sense will not be held up by the franchisor. No one wants to keep an unhappy franchisee.

FINAL WORDS

Starting up a business—even one in which procedures and specifications are almost down to a science—can feel like being on a roller coaster. The ups and downs are completely normal, and as long as you continue to make major decisions methodically and carefully, you will avoid serious problems.

Figure 8.1 Business Structures

Establishment of Business Form and Operation

Proprietorship	Least complicated to create and operate. Not considered a separate legal entity from owner/operator.
General Partnership	Separate legal entity created. Desirable to have formal written agreement regarding all partners. Relatively simple to establish.
Limited Partnership	More complicated than general partnership. Requires written agreement between partners. Creates at least two classes of partners. General partners bear sole responsibility for management.
Regular C Corporation	Separate legal entity that requires formality in creation and operation. May have several classes of shareholders.
S Corporation	Same as regular corporation except restrictions exist regarding types of qualifying shareholders and classes of stock.
Limited Liability Companies	State law varies. Requires formal written agreement. May be treated as a partnership if elected.

Liability for Debts of Business Activity

Proprietorship	Unlimited personal liability exists.
General Partnership	General partners have unlimited liability.
Limited Partnership	Same as general partnership except limited partners generally liable only to the extent of their investment.
S and C Corporations	Stockholders generally liable only to extent of capital investment; however, stockholders may be required to personally guarantee corporate borrowings. In addition, under certain circumstances, "responsible party" stockholders may be liable for non-payment of or under withheld payroll taxes.
Limited Liability Companies	Generally same treatment as limited partnership where all "members" have limited liability.

Deduction of Business Losses by Owners

Proprietorship	Generally, yes. Must be cognizant of "hobby loss" rules.
Partnerships	Yes, Limited Partnership losses usually cannot exceed capital investment. Consider "at risk" rules.
Regular C Corporation	No, losses remain with corporate entity to offset corporate earnings. Loss carryback and carryover provisions exist.
S Corporation	Generally, yes, provided the shareholders have sufficient basis for absorbing losses.
Limited Liability Companies	Generally, yes. Members may deduct losses in accordance with "at risk" provisions.

Federal Income Taxation of Business Profits

Proprietorship	Taxed to individual owner at graduated rates of 15%, 28%, 31% and 36%. Note: In some cases, new 10% surcharge may apply. Also subject to self-employment taxes.
Partnerships	Taxed to partners at individual or corporate rates depending on tax status of partner.
Regular C Corporation	Corporate entity pays tax at graduated rates of 15% on first $50,000 of taxable income, 28% on next $25,000 of taxable income and 34% over $75,000 of taxable income. A 5% surcharge is imposed on taxable incomes over $100,000 to eliminate the benefit of the lower brackets. A higher rate is not imposed on very large corporations.
S Corporation	Generally taxed to individual owners at their respective tax rates. However, in certain cases, a corporate level tax may exist.
Limited Liability Companies	Generally taxed as a partnership.

Potential for Double Taxation upon Withdrawal of Business Profits
(for Federal Tax Purposes)

Proprietorship	None.
Partnerships	None.
Regular C Corporation	Yes, to extent payments exceed reasonable compensation limits to employee/stockholders.
S Corporation	Generally, none.
Limited Liability Companies	Generally, none.

Social Security and Medicare Tax Imposed on Business Profits

Proprietorship	Business profits are taxed at a combined rate of 15.3% applied to "self employment" earnings up to a certain amount. Medicare portion of 2.9% applies without limit. Individual receives a deduction for a portion of this amount in arriving at adjusted gross income.
Partnerships	Self-employment taxes imposed on individual partners on "self-employment earnings" that flow through the partnership. Same limits as proprietorship.
S and C Corporations	Employee/stockholders and corporation on W-2 income share a combined rate of 15.3% equally. There is no Social Security/Medicare tax on profits; however, you must match the employees' withholding portion.
Limited Liability Companies	Generally, same treatment as partnerships.

Retirement Plans

Proprietorship	Keogh Plan, Simplified Employee Pension (SEP) Plan available. Generally same features as corporate and Savings Incentive Match Plan For Employees Plan (SIMPLE) available to unincorporated entities.
Partnerships	Same as for sole proprietorship.
Regular C Corporation	Generally no distinction from plans available to unincorporated entities. Participant borrowings permitted.
S Corporation	Same rules apply as for regular corporations. However, participant borrowings not permitted to 2% or greater shareholder.
Limited Liability Companies	Generally, same as partnerships.

9
FRANCHISE TRENDS AND OPPORTUNITIES

I find that it takes less time to run 11 restaurants—which I manage—rather than one which I used to work in and manage.
DANNY KOSTICK
Pizza Hut franchisee

The 1990s have seen enormous growth and change in franchising, as more and more Americans have decided to try their hand at running their own business. The increasing number of franchisees who are sub-franchisors, area developers or especially multi-unit owners is one trend that will certainly continue. It's probable that by the year 2000 a high percentage of the franchise owners will be owning and operating a sizable corporate entity, rather than the mom-and-pop businesses commonly associated with franchising. Another accelerating trend is the number of independent businesses that convert to a franchise. No doubt you have heard of Century 21, the real estate company. With 7,000 franchised outlets worldwide, Century 21 expands largely by converting existing independent real estate offices to their franchise system. This is a very visible example of conversion franchising. You may be surprised at all the new franchises that are using this technique to expand their businesses.

THE CO-BRANDING TREND

Since the first publication of this book in 1994, the franchise industry has experienced a new phenomenon, which I believe will be the most dominant long-term trend in the industry and one of the best opportunities for franchisees. It's called co-branding. Co-branding can involve two, three or more brands in the same location that complement each other in some way. This way of doing business makes remarkable sense because it not only affords convenience to the customer, but it is also an efficient use of marketing, real estate and facilities for the franchisee owner.

Let's look at some of the ways that co-branding works. The strategy, until now, has been most often employed in the restaurant and food business. Most likely it was first used as a way to even out "day-part" business and seasonal business. I often think of a frozen yogurt franchisee that I interviewed for the first edition of this book. His financial problems stemmed from the fact that his investment in real estate leasing, overhead, employees and marketing were not sufficiently covered because the business almost came to a standstill in the winter months, and, in addition, the bulk of the customers only came to the store during a four- to five-hour period during the day. All this down time was disastrous for his bottom line.

Many of the restaurant/food franchisors have partnered with other food brands for just this reason. The package is especially attractive to its prospective franchisees. One large franchising company, Allied Domeq Retailing USA, has engineered a three-brand opportunity which illustrates how teaming up complementary businesses can be successful. Dunkin' Donuts, the first franchised brand, naturally appeals to the breakfast crowd segment, snackers and some night owls, with its offerings of donuts, bagels and coffee. Baskin-Robbins, the second brand, with its array of ice cream and yogurt flavors, smoothies and other treats, offers snack foods which are eaten from lunch hours up until store closing time. The third brand, the recently acquired Togo's Eatery, a sandwich and salad concept, attracts heavy business at lunch hours and, to a lesser extent, at dinnertime. So, with these three concepts all under one roof, the customer has a good choice of food items at different times of the day, thus allowing the franchisee to take full advantage of her or his capital investment.

Other food franchisors are looking, not only at day-part strategies, but at capturing the consumers' food dollar any way possible. For example, when a customer comes into your fast-food sandwich franchise and the line is long, if you offer a second brand she or he will most likely just move over to the line serving chicken or Mexican food instead of heading out the door. In a group of four or five hungry patrons, it's always an advantage to offer three or more food concepts so that everyone's food preference will be served.

But co-branding is not only for food franchisees. If you are creative, you will think of many pairings that will complement each other. How about a business service set up that combines a computer training franchise with an Internet web site development concept, and, perhaps, an accounting service—all under one roof. Truly, the permutations and possibilities are almost endless.

Tip

If you consider co-branding, do extensive research to ascertain that the two or more concepts have a mix of products or services, operating systems and personnel that meld well and don't duplicate products/services and/or day-parts.

In spite of the recent success of some co-branding arrangements, however, don't view it as the sure road to success. A form of co-branding has experienced only limited success in convenience stores (C-stores). C-stores have jumped on the quick-service restaurant (QSR) bandwagon the last few years in order to bring added profitability to sometimes failing C-stores operations. To be sure, some of the new operations have worked very well, especially some of the mega-centers that offer gasoline and other automotive needs, C-store items and at least one QSR concept. However, combining a retail business and a food operation hasn't been easy for many operators. Operating food-service is very different from operating a C-store. And in many cases where space is a problem, the addition of an express food service with a limited menu has not satisfied customers who expect full menu choices.

Understanding the Terms

Before taking a closer look at the trends, especially those related to "bigger is better," you need to understand the terminology. The following is a brief guide to the most common concepts.

Sub-Franchisor

A franchisee who is granted the right to exercise powers normally reserved for the franchisor—in a specific territory—is a *sub-franchisor*. A separate initial fee is usually charged to the sub-franchisor for the right to sub-franchise an area or territory. Sub-franchisors have the right to offer and sell franchises and to collect fees and royalties. They then have to provide training services and support to franchisees within the boundaries of their designated territories. Like the franchisor, the sub-franchisor signs a sub-franchise agreement with franchisees (when a franchise is sold) in the specified territory.

The fees that are collected by the sub-franchisor may be split between the sub-franchisor and the franchise system, or, in some cases, the sub-franchisor may retain a majority of the fees. The sub-franchise agreement spells out the amount of the franchise fee and royalty each will receive. While this can be an extremely lucrative arrangement for the sub-franchisor, keep in mind that sub-franchisors first have to spend heavily to sign up sub-franchisees in their territories.

Depending on the agreement, the sub-franchisor may operate one unit, several units or no units at all in the territory. Often the development of the territory is subject to a fixed quota or schedule. The expansion objectives may be measured in franchise agreements executed, units open and operating or units "under construction." For example, the agreement may state that within two years after the contract is signed, the sub-franchisor must have a minimum of five units open and operating or lose the exclusive territory. Sub-franchisors can satisfy all or part of their goals by opening units themselves.

Not every franchise system offers sub-franchisor agreements. It does not suit the organization of every franchise business. Then, too, many systems simply don't like the loss of power that goes with sub-franchising. Naturally, sub-franchisors wield more power over the franchisor than do individual franchisees because sub-franchisors control a larger number of units and are responsible for a greater amount of the system's revenue.

From a sub-franchisor's standpoint, the deal isn't always perfect. Sub-franchisors often run a substantial financial risk, since the investment needed to purchase a territory can be large. Also, since sub-franchisors sell franchises, they are exposed to future litigation from disgruntled franchisees. Those risks and headaches, however, are offset by the greater rewards available to sub-franchisors. They will share in both the initial fee for new franchisees, as well as on-going royalty payments, which continue for the life of a franchise agreement—maybe ten or 20 years or more.

Tip

A useful by-product of sub-franchising is a solution to one of the franchisee's biggest challenges—finding and keeping good employees. Stuart and Sharon Ruben signed a sub-franchising agreement for the Money Mailer franchise system, a business of direct mail advertising, not only because they believed they would be able to go out and sell the franchise concept in their territory, but also because they decided the franchisees they signed up would be better motivated to succeed (because their money would be in it) than a number of hired sales people in offices they would be obliged to open in the area.

Area Developers

A franchisee who has the right to establish and operate more than one unit within a defined geographic territory is an *area developer*. Unlike a sub-franchisor, an area developer does not sell or service franchisees in an exclusive area. The area developer will usually pay a fee for the territorial rights and will have a performance obligation or schedule for unit development.

The obligation to open a certain number of units in the designated territory, within a certain period, poses some challenges for area developers. First of all, they must have the financial and managerial capability to develop multiple units. Sometimes, an area agreement will allow the area developer to bring in investors through limited partnerships for the ownership and financing of individual units. However, the area developer remains as the sole general partner.

Aside from financing, questions regarding performance requirements can be the basis for some potential problems. One is the question of units in a territory that are opened and subsequently closed. Are these units counted toward completion of the development schedule? And what happens to the area developer who fulfills performance obligations ahead of schedule? Under most agreements, that developer will be penalized by losing exclusive rights to the territory earlier than expected. One way to avert this problem is to request a right of first refusal for any additional development proposed for your territory. In any case, these points need to be negotiated before the agreement is signed.

Area developers, like sub-franchisors, also wield a great deal of power over the franchisor as compared to individual unit owners. The franchisor will usually try to keep the upper hand by stipulating in the agreement that if performance requirements are not reached by the area developer, the franchise corporation can repurchase the franchise.

Area Representative

This arrangement developed, in part, so that franchisors could have the benefit of sub-franchising without giving up the control that they give up in a sub-franchisor relationship. The *area representative* usually pays the franchisor a fee for the right to solicit prospective franchisees and to provide certain services to existing franchisees in a defined territory. Once an area "rep" finds a new franchisee, the area rep does not enter into contracts with the franchisee, unlike the sub-franchisor. Rather, all franchise agreements are entered into directly between the franchisor and the prospective franchisee. Likewise, the initial fees and royalties are paid directly to the franchisor.

What's in it for the area representative? The franchisor pays the area rep a portion of the initial franchise fees as compensation for finding franchisees (essentially a sales commission) and, if appropriate, a portion of the royalties received for servicing franchisees. In some cases, franchisors will pay area reps a portion of the fee received from new franchisees in the reps' territory even though an area rep had nothing to do with screening or recommending that particular franchisee. Of course, all this and other contingencies—such as compensation for furnishing many of the pre-opening and on-going services to the franchisee—should be covered in the area representation agreement.

Most often the area representative is also a franchisee in the defined territory, owning one or more units. The area rep may own 100% of one unit or may have a smaller ownership in several units.

Linda Moore, previously a senior corporate executive, likes the area representative arrangement she has with Ledger Plus, a franchise that offers accounting, tax planning and tax preparation to small businesses. In particular, she likes that she "is compensated almost immediately for [her] efforts with a cash flow from the beginning." The cash flow comes from the portion of the initial fee and royalties she receives for signing up franchisees. In addition, she says, "I hope to have a steady annuity stream from the on-going royalties I'll be paid. Also, this will be an equity-type business which will be saleable at some time."

When asked about all the time involved in recruiting franchisees, servicing them and operating her own franchise, Linda said, "It's not a problem. In the beginning, most of the work was in recruiting new franchisees for my territory, so there's no support function to worry about. Now, I'm getting into the support function also, but eventually the recruiting will stop and all my efforts [besides running her own franchise] will go to supporting franchisees in my territory."

Linda, coming out of a corporate business background herself, thinks that area representation is a good opportunity for ex-corporate workers to consider. "It provides someone coming from a business development background a way to use her or his skills," she says. Linda adds that she wouldn't want to just sell franchises. It's the whole equation—sales, support and operation of her own franchise—that makes it a rewarding challenge.

Tip

Many single-unit franchise owners complain about not earning enough money. If you have the managerial abilities and the financial resources, owning multiple locations is a way to make a considerable amount of money.

Multiple-Unit Owner

No firm statistics are available as to the number of franchisees who are multiple-unit owners, but a ventured guess is that the number will approach 50% by 2000. Owning and operating more than one unit is clearly a trend and one that most franchise systems are encouraging.

Although the sub-franchisor, the area developer and the area representative may own multiple units, a multiple-unit owner doesn't have to fall into one of these three categories. A multiple unit franchise owner is simply someone who owns and operates more than one location. The multiple-unit owner hires a manager for each of the individual locations and oversees the general management of all the various locations.

Trap

Be very careful that you know exactly what you're doing in the first unit of your franchise business before seriously considering multiple-unit ownership. For example, you should have an efficient accounting system up and running, as well as systems for controlling costs and analyzing sales before you open your second and third locations. As one multiple-unit franchisee found out, "It's difficult to correct bad habits."

It isn't necessary to buy an area or region to open multiple units. If you don't, however, you run the risk of the area you're interested in being taken or saturated by the time you're ready to open a second unit. Sometimes you can avoid these problems by getting a written commitment from the franchisor giving you the right of first refusal to a nearby location that it plans to develop. It's generally easier to get such a commitment from the newer franchise systems.

Tip

Jeff Grayson, a Pizzeria Uno area developer, advises, "Don't buy territories. Open up each restaurant [or unit of whatever the business is] and try to be successful. Focus on each one. Don't be overly concerned about someone else coming in and opening up the same franchise in your area."

Tip

Here's a variation on the multiple-unit ownership you might like to consider: Rather than buy a number of units from the same franchisor, think about buying a variety of franchise businesses in an area or region. For example, you might own and operate five fast-food restaurants, two retail photo shops and three car repair services, all in the same area. In that way, you're diversifying businesses—probably decreasing your financial risk—and building a mini-business empire at the same time.

Master Franchisee

To complete the terminology, a *master franchisee* is actually the same as a sub-franchisor, except on a bigger scale. The term, used in international franchising (an increasingly popular area of franchising), describes a sub-franchisor whose territory is a foreign country or a portion of it. If you are interested in exploring this opportunity, refer to Chapter 10 for details.

CONVERTING AN INDEPENDENT BUSINESS INTO A FRANCHISE UNIT

Converting an existing independent business into a franchised unit of a franchise system is clearly an accelerating trend. Right now about 40% of all franchisors offer conversion franchises.

At the beginning of this chapter, we mentioned Century 21, the real estate company that converts existing businesses to its franchise system. Other real estate concerns, such as Coldwell Banker, Prudential and ERA follow the same strategy. This trend will most likely continue in a variety of businesses.

For example, in this era of the Internet, we can expect to see the organization and structuring of Internet providers, web site technicians and the like into one or several franchise organizations. In general, industries where there is a preponderance of small, independent businesses that can benefit from a centralization of information, an organized marketing strategy and a nationally-known product or service name will be on someone's list for franchising.

A franchised company called MtgPro, headquartered in Rochester, New York, is already doing this with the mortgage brokerage industry. The company brings new technology to a conversion opportunity. In essence, the franchisor recruits independent mortgage brokers and lenders to form an alliance in an effort to better serve the consumer and increase individual lender productivity. The system bills itself as using "21st Century Technology" to develop and maintain its mortgage lending systems. MtgPro uses an Internet-based system called MtgNet, an automated, electronic technology that is applied to all aspects of the lending process. We anticipate that a variety of other franchises will use Internet resources as a means of executing a franchise concept, just as MtgPro is doing, and that many will also be conversion businesses.

In general terms, there are trade-offs for both the franchisee and franchisor in any conversion franchise. For the independent-owner-turned-franchisee, there's the advantage of the franchisor's broader name recognition, the increased marketing and advertising clout and the lower product and supply costs. Those benefits might outweigh the control and independence that the conversion franchisee forfeits. By taking on a conversion franchisee, the franchisor gains an experienced business owner with a track record, while at the same time it loses a competitor. But many franchisors believe they are taking a risk, because it is a very difficult mental adjustment to go from independent to franchisee. Consequently, some conversion franchisees never succeed in making the switch.

Another reason business owners might join a franchise is that the franchisor's product or service is superior to their own. Lisa Brumm was running a bridal dress sales business in Litchfield, Illinois, when she got an invitation to participate in a gown rental convention in Chicago. There she met the owners of Formals Etc., a completely new franchise. She was intrigued by their business idea—renting bridal gowns and other formal wear—so she spent the next six months studying and researching Formals Etc. Lisa came up with three reasons for converting her independent business to a Formals Etc. franchise. First, she wasn't making enough money at her business selling gowns. Second, there was a market need for rentals. And

203

third, her own personal experiences confirmed her gut feeling about the new business. She remembered her husband renting a tux for the numerous weddings where she was a bridesmaid, while she bought a costly dress that she would never wear again. Lisa decided to become a franchisee, and learned quickly that following the franchise system is a necessity, even though she finds that "it's still hard having someone else to answer to."

Sharon Taylor, another conversion franchisee, made the switch for the sake of a new challenge. After 17 years of running an independent bath and soap shop in New Mexico, Sharon decided it was time for a change. At first, she thought about going into a different industry. Then, after looking at a variety of franchises for over a year, she realized she wanted to stay in the body care business, which she already knew. Luckily, she found a franchise that differed only slightly from her previous business, but still offered a change. The franchise, Potions and Lotions, sold private label body care products and custom-made fragrances, did not use animals to test its products, and was committed to recycled packaging. All of this appealed to Sharon. Sharon admits that "it took a lot of mental adjustment to commit myself to pay someone for the idea, pay a royalty and then do all the required paperwork. The process of finally making the decision to buy the franchise was slow and painful."

FINAL WORDS

Franchising, as a business concept, has evolved in the 1990s to accommodate the needs, objectives and talents of the new franchisees for the 21st century. Many new franchisees use a franchise to build a substantial business in which they can utilize all their managerial and technical skills.

10

EXPANDING TO INTERNATIONAL MARKETS

Franchising is not immune to the business cycles, so certainly the current economic problems in Asia will affect the franchising sector there.

PHILIP F. ZEIDMAN

Franchise and Distribution Law at Rudnick, Wolfe, Epstien and
Zeidman

Increasingly, U.S. franchisors are parlaying their expertise and their trademarked concepts in the international arena. Many franchise systems, especially in the restaurant sector, have become dependent on international revenue streams to keep them thriving and profitable. In late 1998, however, economic turmoil in several key foreign regions, such as Russia, parts of Latin America and much of Asia, has caused U.S. franchisors to grow more cautious. The franchise most known for its international expansion, McDonald's, is expected to continue its expansion efforts and will probably continue to succeed because of its experience and strong discipline in overseas operations. But many other systems, without McDonald's resources, are taking a "wait and see" position until conditions improve.

Franchise Hotspots

The top three world regions for U.S. franchisors (outside the U.S.), according to Marcel Portmann, Director of International Development and Global Marketing at the International Franchise Association (IFA), are North America (Canada and Mexico), Western Europe and Latin America. He explains that Canada and Mexico are top choices for expansion because of geographic proximity and language similarity. In fact, Canada is the most popular foreign location for U.S. franchisors, with Mexico as the second most popular. Western Europe is popular because of the sophistication of its market and similarities to the U.S. Latin America is attractive for other reasons. This region has many untapped markets with great potential. In addition, many Latin American nationals travel back and forth to the U.S., so that the franchised brands are already familiar.

Philip Zeidman, a franchise attorney specializing in the international sector at Rudnick, Wolfe, Epstien and Zeidman, basically concurs with Portmann's assessment of key outside markets for U.S. franchisors. His comments on the currently troubled market are worth noting. Regarding the Asiatic regions, Mr. Zeidman says, "Most franchisor clients will defer and restrict their short-term goals for now and may even close some stores, but [they] are not pulling out." The current situation in Russia is perhaps even more troubled, and as a result Mr. Zeidman doesn't envision any franchisor going into Russia in order to open its first store in the near future.

New international growth markets for the longer term are China and India, according to Zeidman. He says, "China is probably the biggest growth market for our lifetime." He believes any major franchise company will put China at the top of its list. India also shows great promise for franchise expansion because of its status as the second largest market in the world. Besides the fact that English is the common business language in India, a rising middle-income population of about 150–250 million can't be ignored. The country still hasn't completely shaken off 50 years of bureaucracy, however, and this can cause a multitude of problems for both the franchisor and master franchisee.

The biggest change in international franchise markets, according to Zeidman, is the proliferation of franchise litigation. Only a few years ago, there was little franchise regulation outside the U.S. However, laws to regulate franchising are now being put forth in countries like Japan, Korea, Australia, Indonesia and Malaysia.

To get an idea of the number of franchisors, operating both in the U.S. and other countries, refer to Figure 10.1 at the end of this chapter. The charts are part of a study conducted by Arthur Andersen and Co. in 1995 under the direction of the International Franchise Association.

Tip

Most of the international franchise market is where the United States was ten or 15 years ago. Global opportunities are plentiful.

CANDIDATES FOR INTERNATIONAL FRANCHISING

This book will be read in many countries outside of the U.S. If you are an individual living in a country other than the United States, you will find information in this chapter which will help you understand the mechanics and special considerations of buying a U.S. franchise for operation in your country. You may also consider buying native franchise systems, which are fairly well-represented in Canada and Western Europe.

Tip

For individuals seeking permanent resident status (PRS) in the United States, there is now a way to combine an interest in franchising with PRS. The 1990 U.S. Immigration Act created a new category of immigrant visas. Under the act's provisions, a foreign citizen who buys a franchise in the United States may receive the "green card" which provides PRS.

It requires an investment of $500,000–$3 million, depending on location and regional unemployment conditions. For those unable to invest $500,000, one could qualify for the E-2 visa or "treaty investor." This requires a "substantial" investment, but not necessarily $500,000. In addition, the capital that is invested must directly benefit the U.S. economy and employ at least ten U.S. citizens.

If you are interested in these business visas and have a desire to purchase a U.S. franchise, you should contact the U.S. embassy in your country or a company on the Internet at greencardusa.com.

THE IDEAL INTERNATIONAL FRANCHISEE

The franchising relationship is often likened to a marriage. This comparison is heightened in the international franchise relationship, where a lengthy courting and engagement period normally precedes the ultimate "marriage." Some franchisors and franchisees are even asking for test period arrangements, of, say, one or two years, before the final franchise agreement is signed.

The procedures can be painstaking because the stakes are big in international franchising. The franchise relationship, as we noted in the previous chapter, is usually that of a franchisor and a master franchisee. The territory that is licensed to the master franchisee is not a zip code area or a portion of a state, instead, the licensed area is quite often an entire country or a large portion of one.

Tip

The most attractive candidates for international franchising, from the point of view of the franchisor, are those who already own or lease good locations.

In general terms, these are the qualities and requirements the franchisor will be looking for in a master franchisee:

❧ The master franchisee should know the local market. This includes the culture, real estate opportunities, suppliers, financial institutions and relevant laws and regulations.

❧ Ideally, the franchisee will have experience in the industry or business that is being franchised. In lieu of this, knowledge of and successful experience in a general business area are usually acceptable.

❧ Proven financial resources are a necessity. The master franchisee must have the wherewithal (either alone or most commonly with other investors) to buy the franchise rights, set up prototypes and systems and develop the concept in the agreed upon territory.

❧ Proven management skills are another necessity. For the most part, the master franchisee will be functioning just as the franchise system does in its native country. That requires management skills in such areas as sales and marketing, training and operations.

❧ The master franchisee should be enthusiastic and convinced about the feasibility of the franchisor's concept and system. Wanting to "do it your way" is a red flag to the franchisor.

❧ The franchisor looks for a certain "chemistry" in its master franchisee, which can be defined in part as integrity and a cooperative attitude.

Tip

If you have your sights set on a U.S. franchise—and you are a national of another country—the franchisor will require that you be able to communicate well in English.

Tip

Be careful when translating U.S. slogans, advertising copy and the like into a foreign language. For example, in Chinese, the KFC slogan "finger-lickin' good" translates as "Eat your fingers off."

FINDING THE INTERNATIONAL FRANCHISE

If you are a national of the United States, Canada or the United Kingdom, for example, and have an interest in a native franchise system for export to another country, you'll find the franchise the same way as you would for a domestic venture. You'll attend franchise shows, read the publications that list all the operating franchise systems, and talk to franchisees in your area.

Finding the right franchise when you are a native of, say, Hong Kong or Brazil and would like to operate a U.S. franchise in your country is a little more difficult. Here are some of the ways to locate the perfect franchise when operating from a distance:

- The International Herald Tribune *International Franchise Guide* is the most up-to-date and comprehensive annual directory of franchisors who want to promote their systems internationally. There is a very detailed profile on each of the companies, including specific countries where they wish to expand. The *IHT Guide* also includes information on international franchise attorneys, consultants, etc. .

- In foreign countries, the U.S. embassy offers a commercial service that helps local nationals learn about U.S. business opportunities. A "Gold Key" program offered by the embassy registers a foreign national and notes the specifics of the business interest (e.g., computer learning, printing) and the amount of the investment. The Commerce Desk then tries to match the prospective buyer with appropriate businesses. In the case of franchising, the franchisor might send high-level management to your country to discuss the opportunity.

    Contact a reputable franchise consultant who can set up meetings with viable and pre-screened franchise systems that fit your qualifications. A fee is charged for this service, but it may save you much time and effort.

    Franchise expos are held in almost every major city in the world. This is a good way to survey the international franchise opportunities and follow up on the ones that interest you.

    The International Franchise Association (IFA) holds conferences where a variety of international franchise opportunities are presented by the principals of the company in locations around the world. These conferences are usually supported by major media advertising and publications such as the Asian *Wall Street Journal* and the *International Herald Tribune*.

    Contact your national franchise association. Although not every country has one, most of the countries with strong franchising development have active associations. (See the Appendix for a listing of franchise associations.)

FORMS OF INTERNATIONAL FRANCHISING

Although most franchise systems prefer a master franchise set-up for their international expansion, other forms of agreements are sometimes chosen. These formats include the single-unit franchise, the area development agreement or a joint venture agreement.

Master Franchise. In this arrangement, the master franchisee (also called the "sub-franchisor") is granted a franchise for all or part of a target country. The master franchisee, which may be an individual, a group or a company, has the right to develop the entire territory or sub-franchise the units to third parties (sub-franchisees).

The franchisor trains the master franchisee. In turn, the master franchisee recruits and trains sub-franchisees to operate individual units of the franchise in their country. In effect, the master franchisee is now the franchisor in that country and receives a portion of the royalties for its support of individual franchises.

Area Development Franchise. Similar to a master franchise agreement, a person, group or company gains the right to develop an entire country or part of it. However, unlike the master franchise, the focus is on running the business, not selling franchises. Substantial capital and management resources are necessary for the area developer, since there will be no sub-franchisees to share the risks and capital requirements.

Single-Unit Franchise. U.S. franchises rarely sanction a single unit outside the country with the possible exceptions of Canada and Mexico (because of their proximity). In this case, a franchisee obtains the rights to open a unit of the franchise in her or his native country. Franchisors steer away from this type of arrangement because of the great costs sustained in servicing one unit outside the country.

Joint Ventures. Two parties, the franchisor and the sub-franchisor, make contributions to the investment in this arrangement. The parties negotiate their ownership shares and decide how to finance their contributions. The franchisors often contribute expertise, a system and sometimes cash. The foreign partners may contribute money and local knowledge. In essence, the joint venture company becomes the sub-franchisor.

Franchise systems will usually not consider a joint venture arrangement, which puts their own capital at risk, unless the country is one they want to enter and they can't do it any other way. This is most common in Eastern European countries, where the markets are promising, but potential franchisees do not have the capital to totally fund the investment.

CHECKLIST FOR CHOOSING AN INTERNATIONAL FRANCHISE BUSINESS

These are the basic questions you should be able to answer before getting down to serious negotiations with the franchisor.

Preliminary

1. Is there any regulation of foreign investments in your target country? Find out the details.

2. Are there any local laws and restrictions that would prohibit certain types of franchises?

3. Are there any import restrictions or laws governing the kinds of products or services that you can source from outside the country?

More Specific

4. Is there already an established demand for the franchise product or service? (It is very risky and expensive to try and create a demand where one does not already exist.)

5. Does the franchise have at least minimal name recognition? (The franchisor should have at least 25 outlets in a concentrated area.)

6. Is the franchise system financially strong and stable? (Companies looking for a quick buck will fail. The franchisor must commit to a longer pay-out period for international franchising.)

7. Is the system and the mind set of the franchise management flexible? (Often a part of the system has to be changed for a foreign market.)

8. Does the business have unique features that will give it an edge over the competition?

9. Are suppliers of the components, ingredients, equipment or other needs of the business readily available?

10. Is the franchise trademark registered and protected in the target country?

Tip

Trademark protection is crucial for success. However, a franchise company frequently finds that its trademark has already been filed by someone else in the foreign country. This occurs because, unlike in the United States, prior use is not a prerequisite for registration in many countries.

Japan is an example of a difficult market in which to register a trademark. An illustration occurred in the 1970s when a lawyer for McDonald's attempted to register the company's famous "golden arches" trademark. He found that a Japanese food distributor had registered the trademark just one day earlier. McDonald's finally obtained the right to use the golden arches, but the ownership of the trademark is still in doubt.

Accordingly, it is essential that you determine whether or not the trademark is protected in your target country. Not only is this a prerequisite for you to do business, but you, as the franchisee, may be asked to pay for part of the buy-back amount if the franchisor has to buy back a trademark from "pirates."

Contract Provisions

The details of the contract will vary with the type of agreement which is reached, i.e., master franchise, single unit, area development or joint venture. As you can imagine, a joint venture agreement can get very lengthy and complicated, since responsibilities and obligations for the two parties must be carefully spelled out. Engaging a competent franchise attorney is an absolute necessity in a joint venture agreement, as well as any of the other international franchise formats.

Since the vast majority of international franchise agreements are master franchise set ups, that is our focus. We will concentrate on the singular elements of an international agreement, and you should refer to Chapters 4 and 5 for the basics, which remain the same for both domestic and international agreements.

Initial Master Franchise Fees

Initial licensing fees are very often a source of conflict for the franchisor and the master franchisee. The challenge is to negotiate a fee, generally ranging from a low of $50,000 to over $1 million, which will reconcile the interests of the two parties.

The franchisor will probably insist on a substantial initial fee for all or some of the following reasons:

- The franchisor will be giving up the right to open outlets or grant the franchises to a third party. The system wants compensation for the lost development opportunity.

❧ The international agreement will be costly to the franchisor in terms of financial and human resources. Some of the costs incurred are: initial training of the sub-franchisor and representatives; travel and living expenses for company executives sent to train and assist sub-franchisors in the target country and possible replacements for these executives in the home country; and the registration of trademarks, translation of documents and sales materials and assorted legal fees.

❧ The franchisor believes that a substantial fee will ensure that the sub-franchisor is committed to the success of the franchise system in the target country.

The perspective of the sub-franchisor is, of course, different. It will want to pay the smallest initial fee possible for the following reasons:

❧ The sub-franchisor will assume the greater financial risk. Apart from the initial franchise fee, the sub-franchisor will also have the following expenses: opening up a number of franchise outlets before enlisting sub-franchises; establishing a training facility for sub-franchisees; acquiring land and buildings or leasing the premises with a long-term liability; and paying for the training, transportation, lodging and meals of senior executives in the franchisor's country.

❧ The sub-franchisor is exposed to significant business risk, since the franchise system is untested in the target country. In addition, the name recognition of the product or service may be non-existent in the sub-franchisor's home country.

❧ Depending on negotiations, the cost of the market research, translations of materials and other similar obligations may be assumed in whole or in part by the sub-franchisor.

Development Schedule

The rate at which franchise outlets will open is also an area of conflict for the franchisor and the international sub-franchisor. It is in the franchisor's interest to demand an aggressive development schedule, whereas the sub-franchisor will want a conservative one. Expect prolonged negotiations before coming to an agreement on this question.

The franchisor feels justified in requiring that the sub-franchisor open up the largest number of outlets in the smallest amount of time, since the company is giving up its development rights in the target country. Development of the market is controlled by the sub-franchisor.

The sub-franchisor, however, will not want to increase its financial and business risk by agreeing to an aggressive development schedule. An additional concern is that franchise outlets will be opened in secondary locations in order to keep up with the schedule, increasing the likelihood of the failure of the entire business.

USING A TEST PERIOD AGREEMENT

One of the ways to help reconcile the opposing viewpoints of franchisor and sub-franchisor is to enter into a test period agreement. The sub-franchisor is granted the right and license in the exclusive territory with the obligation of opening a specified number of franchise outlets within a certain period of time. But the master franchise agreement is only entered into if the results of the test period are positive. The initial fee is not paid until a master franchise agreement is signed.

Test Period Agreement

If a test period agreement is utilized, other issues will have to be addressed. For example, who decides whether the master franchise agreement will be instituted? The franchisor or the sub-franchisor can decide to go ahead or the decision can be mutual (Negotiate for the right to make the decision!). Alternatively, the decision could depend on previously agreed upon criteria—such as outlets opened or sales volume achieved—which, if met, commit both parties to the execution of the master franchise agreement.

Since there is no master franchise agreement during the test period, the sub-franchisor will usually enter into a unit franchise agreement for each unit opened. The standard single unit agreement used in the home country can be utilized with, probably, a few adaptations. Some of these include voiding a payment of the initial unit fee (the initial master fee will be paid when the master franchise agreement is concluded), reduced royalty payments or none at all, and a different level of franchisor service.

The level and cost of training and assistance by the franchisor are issues that must also be negotiated. Usually, the franchisor will provide initial training, which includes pre-opening, opening and post-opening assistance free of charge. Travel and hotel expenses associated with the training are sometimes paid by the sub-franchisor.

The franchisor will usually require that the sub-franchisor maintain strict confidentiality on proprietary information and know-how that is given to the sub-franchisor during the test period. In the event that the master franchise agreement is not signed, the sub-franchisor may be required to agree to not carry on a competing business.

The test period term is generally for a period of 1 or 2 years. The sub-franchisor should allow sufficient time to make reasonable as-sessment of the viability of the franchise system in the target country. Negotiate for more time if you think you need it.

The master franchise agreement will, in all probability, cover an entire country. For the test period, the sub-franchisor should limit the territory to a small region or a city.

Decide who will be in charge of advertising and promotion in the country during the test period. With a master franchise agreement, usually the sub-franchisor is in charge of those areas.

Tip

Negotiate all the provisions of the master franchise agreement and attach it to the test period agreement so that there are no surprises when the test period ends.

Outcome of the Test Period

If there is a decision not to proceed with the master franchise agreement, a few matters will have to be dealt with. One of these is the ownership of the resulting data and knowledge. It is customary that all such knowledge and know-how remain the exclusive property of the franchisor, but, in special instances, the parties may agree to a joint ownership.

Then there's the question of what to do with the franchise outlets that have been opened. Various possibilities may be considered. Often the unit franchise agreements are terminated and the outlets are liquidated with no trace of the franchise business remaining. This can be extremely costly for the sub-franchisor, especially when land and buildings have been purchased and leasehold improvements made. Negotiate the cost of liquidation with the franchisor in the test period agreement and at least try for shared costs.

Another alternative is for the sub-franchisor to operate the franchise outlets under the terms of each unit franchise agreement. No further expansion would be necessary, and a master franchise agreement would not be signed. If the sub-franchisor decides not to operate the outlets, the agreement might allow the franchisor to buy the outlets on the basis of a pre-determined price or formula. The franchisor might then develop the territory itself or grant a master franchise to a third party.

If the test period is positive, the parties will enter into a master franchise agreement. At this point the sub-franchisor is required to pay the initial master franchise fee. On the positive side, the sub-franchisor has tested the system and has reduced the risk to an acceptable level. From the point of view of the franchisor, however, a resulting positive test period can justify an increased initial fee and require a more aggressive development schedule.

Tip

All factors considered, my advice is to negotiate a test period agreement for any and all franchise businesses before finalizing a master franchise agreement.

FINANCING THE PROJECT

Financing your international franchise investment, just like a domestic one, will be a challenge. And, since we're talking in terms of developing an entire country market, the numbers will be much larger and the time spent in putting together the financial package will be considerable. Usually, a consortium or a group of individuals invests in a master franchise or area development agreement. It is rare that an individual will be able to finance and develop an international investment alone.

Tip

Most franchisors are not interested in individuals who put together an international deal using other people's money and contribute nothing themselves. Franchisors want successful entrepreneurs who will put their own money on the line.

Trap

Beware. All successful franchise ideas don't transfer, and it's not always easy to pick the winners. Consider this experience in Belgium: KFC didn't work well in Belgium, and the natives didn't even want to try the frozen yogurt franchise products, but Chi-Chi's, a full-service Mexican restaurant franchise, is doing great!

Some of the international banking institutions have developed franchising investment departments as an integral part of their business. Two of these are The Royal Bank of Scotland and the Generale De Banque in Brussels, Belgium. The franchising officer in the Brussels bank, Mr. Fons Durinck, contends that the bank will try to finance international franchise agreements whenever possible.

Ex-Im Bank Program

In September of 1997, the Export-Import Bank of the United States (Ex-Im Bank) announced a program to support franchising. The Bank's short- and medium-term programs for the support of financing U.S. goods and service exports are available to overseas franchises and U.S. franchisors. It is envisioned that most of the support will be under Ex-Im Bank's Insurance Program.

Under this program, franchise fees are eligible on a case-by-case basis. If the fee represents an equity investment, it is ineligible, as are royalties and other periodic fees. Capital equipment is eligible for support if it meets U.S. content standards. Stocking and restocking needs are eligible for Ex-Im's short-term insurance support.

If you are closing an agreement on a U.S. franchise system, ask the franchisor about the possibility of utilizing Ex-Im's program. In addition, three other U.S. Government agencies also support franchising. They are: the Overseas Private Investment Corporation, the U.S. Small Business Administration and the U.S. Aid Office of Investment. Contact information on Ex-Im Bank and other U.S. government agencies is located in the Appendix.

AN AMERICAN IN HUNGARY

George Hemingway is the managing director of Hemingway Holding AG, a public company that operates a variety of international businesses, some of which are franchises. Hemingway started out by buying companies in Hungary, businesses as diverse as gourmet shops and agricultural publishing. Several years ago, the company concluded master franchise agreements for Hungary with the Dunkin' Donuts, KFC and Pizza Hut franchise systems.

Hemingway says he saw an opportunity and acted on it. The McDonald's franchise was opening in Hungary, but no others seemed imminent, so he started talking to franchise systems that he thought would work in the country. Hemingway, though, wasn't starting cold. His company was already operating businesses in Hungary, so he was familiar with the culture, work habits and problems of doing business in a former Soviet-bloc country. In fact, Hemingway, with an office in Los Angeles, found it a necessity to spend over 50% of his time in Hungary to oversee the businesses.

The financing for the franchises was put together in the United States. The Hungarian government, says Hemingway, didn't give any financial help, although Hemingway could have obtained loans with very high rates. Hungarian nationals, however, are eligible for lower rate enterprise loans.

Hemingway and his group negotiated obligations and performance objectives with each of the franchise systems. The company's longer term plan is to sub-franchise to Hungarian nationals and set up local training centers for the sub-franchisees.

In spite of the cultural differences, adapting the franchises for the Hungarian population wasn't too difficult. The food and preparation stayed pretty much the same. A three-month supply of food was sent from the United States for the franchise unit's opening, but company plans called for eventually having 100% of the food supply produced in Hungary.

Hemingway did find that the decor and interiors of the franchise units had to be upgraded. An upscale look was necessary because the prices in the outlets are higher than Hungarian-owned food outlets. A fancier decor was a way to justify paying more, and it is something the local population craved. Hemingway gave local artists the job of decorating the outside and inside of the buildings, complete with murals. Most certainly, the Pizza Hut in Budapest, with its elaborate Hollywood-style décor, is successful, and the lines of customers often stretch out onto the street. The other franchise units will continue the upscale image.

One key to this group's success is their acquisition of prime real estate locations prior to negotiating the franchise agreements. The company, Hemingway stated, still has good locations in its inventory for further site development.

FINAL WORDS

Experienced entrepreneurs will find international franchising a challenging and rewarding opportunity. The risks are greater than for domestic ventures, but the payoff with a successful operation can be substantial.

Figure 10.1 Franchisor Distribution throughout World

- ֍ On average, there are 333 franchisors per country (252 not including the U.S.).

- ֍ The number of franchisors per country given above may also include both U.S. franchisors and franchisors of other countries.

- ֍ 44% of the countries have 200 or more franchisors.

- ֍ 56% of the countries have less than 200 franchisors.

- ֍ The number of franchisors per country ranges from 0 to 3,000 (U.S.).

Number of Franchisors per Country
(Less Than 200 per Country)

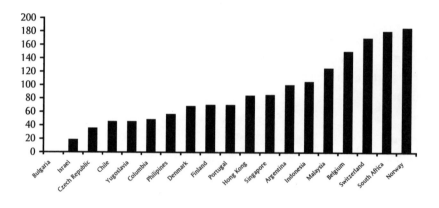

Number of Franchisors per Country
(More Than 200 per Country)

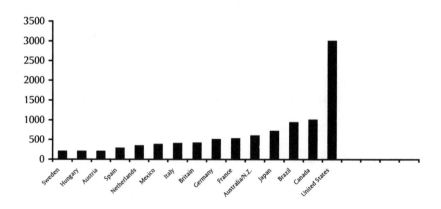

Source: Arthur Andersen & Co. SC, 1995

Appendix

Selected Contacts for Franchise Information

General Contact Organization
International Franchise Association
1350 New York Ave., NW, # 900
Washington, DC 20005
Tel: 202-628-8000
Fax: 202-628-0812
Web Site: www.franchise.org
Contact: Mr. Don J. DeBolt, President
Ms. Debbie Smith, Vice President of
Research, Minority and Women's Affairs

International Franchise Association Organization Members (Source: International Franchise Association)

Argentina Franchise Association
Av. Liberator 222, 7 piso-A
Buenos Aires, 1001 ARGENTINA
Contact: Mrs. Veronica Liendo
Tel: 54-11-4394-3318
Fax: 54-11-4326-5499
www.aafranchising.com

Australia Franchise Council
Level 14/461 Bourke St.
Melbourne, 300 AUSTRALIA
Contact: Mr. Jim McCracken
Tel: 61-03-9650-1667
Fax: 61-03-9650-1713
www.fca.com.au

Brazil Franchise Association
Avenida Brigadeiron Faria Lima,
1.739 Jardim Paulistano
Sao Paulo, CEP01452-001 BRAZIL
Contact: Ms. Anette Trompeter
Tel: 55-11-38-14-4200
Fax: 55-11-38-17-5986
www.abf.com.br

British Franchise Association
Thames View, Newtown Rd.
Henley on Thames
Oxforshire, RG9 1HG GREAT BRITAIN
Contact: Mr. Brian Smart
Tel: 44-1491-578-050
Fax: 44-1491-573-517
www.british-franchise.org.uk

Canadian Franchise Association
2585 Skymark Ave., # 300
Mississauga, ON L4W 4L5 CANADA
Contact: Mr. Richard Cunningham
Tel: 905-625-2896
Fax: 905-625-9076
www.cfa.ca

European Franchise Federation
Boulevard de l'Humanite 116/2
Brussels B-1070 BELGIUM
Contact: Ms. Carol Chopra
Tel: 32-2-520-1607
Fax: 32-2-520-1735

French Franchise Federation
60, Rue La Boetie
Paris, 75008 FRANCE
Contact: Ms. Chantal Zimmer
Tel: 33-1-53-75-22-25
Fax: 33-1-53-75-22-20
www.franchise-fff.com

German Franchise Assocation
Paul Heyse St., 33-35
Munchen, 80336 GERMANY
Contact: Mr. Utho Creusen
Tel: 49-89-53-07-140
Fax: 49-89-53-13-23

Hong Kong Franchise Association
22/F Unit A United Centre
95 Queensway HONG KONG
Contact: Ms. Charlotte Chow
Tel: 852-2529-9229
Fax: 852-2527-9843
www.franchise.org.hk

Ibero American Franchise Federation (FIAF)
Avda. de las Ferias S/N
46035 Valencia SPAIN

Contact: Mr. Xavier Vallhonrat
Tel: 34-96-386-1123
Fax: 34-96-363-6111

Italian Franchise Association
Corso di Porta Nuova, 3
Milano, 20121 ITALY
Contact: Mr. Michele Scardi
Tel: 39-02-2900-3779
Fax: 39-02-655-5919
www.assofranchising.it

Japan Franchise Association
2nd Akiyama Bldg.
Toranomon 3-6-2 Minato-ku
Tokyo 105-0001 JAPAN
Contact: Mr. Isao Seo
Tel: 81-3-03-5777-8704
Fax: 81-3-03-5777-8711

Mexico Franchise Association
Insurgentes Sur 1783, # 303
Mexico, DF 01020 MEXICO
Contact: Mr. Fernando Rocha Huerta
Tel: 52-5-661-0655
Fax: 52-5-663-2473

New Zealand Franchise Association
P.O. Box 25650
St. Heliers, Auckland NEW ZEALAND
Contact: Mr. Winston Robinson
Tel: 64-9-575-3804
Fax: 64-9-575-3807

Philippines Franchise Association
2/F Collins Bldg., 167 EDSA
Mandaluyong City PHILIPPINES
Contact: Ma. Alegria S. Limjoco
Tel: 63-2-532-6777
Fax: 63-2-532-5644

Singapore Franchise Association
5 International Business Park, Informatics Bldg.
609914 SINGAPORE
Contact: Mr. Robert Leong
Tel: 65-568-0802
Fax: 65-568-0722

South Africa Franchise Association
24 Wellington Rd.
2193 Houghton, 2041 SOUTH AFRICA
Contact: Mr. Nic Louw
Tel: 27-11-484-1285
Fax: 27-11-484-1291
www.fasa.co.za

Spain Franchise Association
Avda. de las Ferias S/N,
P.O. Box 476
Valencia, 46035 SPAIN
Contact: Mr. Eduardo Abadia
Tel: 34-96-386-1123
Fax: 34-96-363-6111

Franchise Show Schedules
MFV
210 East Rte. 4, # 403
Paramus, NJ 07652
Tel: 201-226-1130
Fax: 201-226-1131

Franchise Consultants and Research
FranchiseHelp, Inc.
101 Executive Blvd., 2nd Floor
Elmsford, NY 10523
Tel: 914-347-6735
Fax: 914-347-4063
Contact: Mary E. Tomzack
E-mail: mtomzack@bestweb.net
Internet: www.franchisehelp.com

Franchise Attorneys
Fisher Schumacher Zucker LLC
121 S. Avenue of the Arts,
1200
Philadelphia, PA 19107
Tel: 215-545-5200
Contact: Mr. Joseph Shumacher
Mr. Lane Fisher

Harold L. Kestenbaum, P.C.
585 Stewart Ave., # 700
Garden City, NY 11530
Tel: 516-745-0999

Loeb & Loeb LLP
1000 Wilshire Blvd., # 1800
Los Angeles, CA 90017-2475
Tel: 213-688-3786
Contact: Mr. Kenneth R. Costello

Rudnick, Wolfe, Epstein & Zeidman
1201 NY Ave.
Washington, DC 20005
Tel: 202-712-7200
Contact: Mr. Phil Zeidman
Mr. Bret Lowell

Lending Sources
American Commercial Capital
5963 La Place Ct., # 300
Carlsbad, CA 92008-8823
Tel: 760-918-2700

Amresco, Inc.
3010 LBJ Freeway, # 920
Dallas, TX 75234
Tel: 972-247-1776

AT&T/Newcourt Capital Corp.
44 Whippany Rd.
Morristown, NJ 07962
Tel: 800-221-7252

AT&T/Newcourt Financial
11350 Random Hills Rd., # 800
Fairfax, VA 22030
Tel: 703-934-6052

Atherton Capital, Inc.
1001 Bayhill Dr., # 155
San Bruno, CA 94066
Tel: 650-827-7800

Banco Popular
7 W. 51st St.
New York, NY 10019
Tel: 212-315-2800

Capital Expressway, Inc.
10565 Brunswick Rd., # 11
Grass Valley, CA 95945
Tel: 800-913-9119

CAPTEC Financial Group
24 Frank Lloyd Wright Dr.
Ann Harbor, MI 48108
Tel: 313-994-5505

Citibank NA
450 Mamaroneck Ave.
Harrison, NY 10528-2401
Tel: 914-899-7657

Citicorp
2600 Michaelson Dr.
Irvine, CA 92612
Tel: 714-250-6489

Commercial Capital Corporation
8000 Bonhomme Ave., # 217
St. Louis, MO 63105
Tel: 314-721-3131

Deutsche Bank Securities
Franchise Lending Group

31 W. 52nd St., 17th Floor
New York, NY 10019
Tel: 212-469-3886

FINOVA Capital
115 W. Century Rd.
Paramus, NJ 07652
Tel: 201-634-3312

Franchise Mortgage Acceptance Corporation
Five Greenwich Office Park
Greenwich, CT 06831
Tel: 800-884-3622

Franchise Mortgage Acceptance Corporation
1888 Century Park, E, 3rd Floor
Los Angeles, CA 90067
Tel: 800-611-3622

Franchise Finance Corporation of America
17207 N. Perimeter Dr.
Scottsdale, AZ 85255
Tel: 800-528-1179

GreenTree Franchise Finance
7360 South Kyrene Rd.
Tempe, AZ 85283
Tel: 888-513-8733

GreenTree Franchise Finance
One Pierce Pl., # 512
Itasca, IL 60143
Tel: 800-322-0444

GreenTree Franchise Finance
3601 MN Dr., # 900
Bloomington, MN 55435
Tel: 612-837-2000

Heller Financial
1625 Broadway, # 1800
Denver, CO 80202
Tel: 303-592-8125

International Franchise Capital
3900 5th Ave., # 340
San Diego, CA 92103
Tel: 888-432-0432

Lexington Capital Corporation
420 Lake Cook Rd.
Deerfield, IL 60015
Tel: 800-532-7353

Peachtree Franchise Finance
2859 Paces Ferry Rd., # 1760
Atlanta, GA 30339
Tel: 888-81-PEACH (73224)

Phoenix Leasing Inc.
2401 Kerner Blvd.
San Rafael, CA 94901
Tel: 800-521-4054

PMC Capital Inc.
17920 Preston Rd.
Dallas, TX 75252
Tel: 800-486-3223

Sanwa Business Credit Corporation
One South Wacker Dr.
Chicago, IL 60606-4614
Tel: 312-853-1249

SunTrust Credit
111 Center St., # 1000
Little Rock, AR 72201
Tel: 800-395-7077

Textron Financial, Corporation
40 Westminster St.

Providence, RI 02904
Tel: 800-343-0053

The Money Store
3301 C St., # 100-M
Sacramento, CA 95816
Tel: 916-554-8401

The Money Store Investment Corp.
220 Commerce Dr., # 230
Fort Washington, PA 19034
Tel: 215-641-9660

The Money Store Investment Corp.
384 Inverness Dr., S, # 204
Englewood, CO 80112
Tel: 303-792-0363

U.S. Restaurant Lending Group
5310 Harvest Hill, # 270 LB168
Dallas, TX 75230
Tel: 972-387-1487

U.S.A. Capital
88 Steele St., # 400
Denver, CO 80206
Tel: 303-270-9382

Federal Government Small Business
Sources
General:
U.S. Small Business Administration
409 3rd St., SW, Room 7177
Washington, DC 20416
Tel: 202- 606-4000 ext. 296 Answer Desk
Web Site: www.sba.gov

SBA regional offices: The SBA has offices located throughout the United States. For the one nearest you, look under "U.S. Government" in your telephone directory, or call the SBA Answer Desk at (800) 8-ASK-

SBA. To send a Fax to the SBA, dial (202) 205-7064. For the hearing impaired, the TDD number is (704) 344-6640.

Agencies and Organizations to find a Small Business Investment Company (SBIC):

U.S. Small Business Administration
Associate Administrator for Investment
Washington, DC 20416
Tel: 202-205-6510
Fax: 202-205-6959
Web Site: www.sbaonline.sba.gov/inv. (for a state by state listing of SBICs)

The National Association of Small Business Investment Companies (NASBIC)
666 11th St., NW, # 750
Washington, DC 20001
Tel: 202-628-5055
E-mail: nasbic@nasbic.org.

Offers publications that can help small business owners find an SBIC and complete the financing process.

The National Association of Investment Companies (NAIC)
1111 14th St., NW, # 700
Washington, DC 20005
Tel: 202-289-4336
Web Site: www.envista.com/naic.

Publishes a membership directory that can be obtained at the above address.

Business Development Resources for Minorities and Women
U.S. Department of Commerce, Minority Business Development Agency (MBDA)
Room 5055

14th and Constitution Ave., NW
Washington, DC 20230
Tel: 202-482-5061
Fax: 202-501-6137
Web Site: www. mbda.doc.gov

The MBDA regional or district offices are broken into regions:
Atlanta region (Alabama, Florida, Georgia, Kentucky, Mississippi, North Carolina, Puerto Rico, South Carolina, Tennessee, Virgin Islands):

MBDA Regional Office
401 West Peachtree St., NW, # 1715
Atlanta, GA 30308
Tel: 404-730-3300
Fax: 404-730-3313

MBDA District Office
51 S.W. First Ave.
Room 1314, Box 25
Miami, FL 33130
Tel: 305-536-5054
Fax: 305-530-7068

Chicago region (Illinois, Indiana, Iowa, Kansas, Michigan, Minnesota, Missouri, Nebraska, Ohio, Wisconsin):
MBDA Regional Office
55 E. Monroe St., # 1406
Chicago, IL 60603
Tel: 312-353-0182
Fax: 312-353-0191

Dallas region (Arkansas, Colorado, Louisiana, Montana, New Mexico, North Dakota, Oklahoma, South Dakota, Texas, Utah, Wyoming):
MBDA Regional Office
1100 Commerce St., Room 7B-23
Dallas, TX 75242
Tel: 214-767-8001
Fax: 214-767-0613

New York region (Connecticut, Delaware, Maine, Maryland, Massachusetts, New Hampshire, New Jersey, New York, Pennsylvania, Rhode Island, Vermont, Washington, DC, West Virginia):

MBDA Regional Office
26 Federal Plaza, Room 3720
New York, NY 10278
Tel: 212-264-3262
Fax: 212-264-0725

MBDA District Office
10 Causeway St., # 418
Boston, MA 02222-1041
Tel: 617-565-6850
Fax: 617-565-8897

MBDA District Office
600 Arch St.
Room 10128
Philadelphia, PA 19106
Tel: 215-597-9236
Fax: 215-597-1994

San Francisco region (Alaska, American Samoa, Arizona, California, Hawaii, Idaho, Nevada, Oregon, Washington):

MBDA Regional Office
221 Main St.
Room 1280
San Francisco, CA 94105
Tel: 415-744-3001
Fax: 415-744-3061

MBDA District Office
9660 Flair Dr.
El Monte, CA 91731
Tel: 818-453-8636
Fax: 818-453-8640

INDEX

Definitive Franchisor Database
Available for Rent

SAMPLE FRANCHISOR PROFILE

Name of Franchise:	AARON'S SALES & LEASE OWNERSHIP
Address:	309 East Paces Ferry Rd., N. E.
City/State/Zip/Postal Code:	Atlanta, GA 30305-2377
Country:	U. S. A.
800 Telephone #:	(800) 551-6015
Local Telephone #:	(404) 237-4016
Alternate Telephone #:	
Fax #:	(404) 240-6540
E-Mail:	jim.steger@aaronsfranchise.com
Internet Address:	www.aaronsfranchise.com
# Franchised Units:	186
# Company-Owned Units:	238
# Total Units:	424
Company Contact:	Mr. Jim Steger
Contact Title/Position:	Director of Franchise Development
Contact Salutation:	Mr. Steger
President:	Mr. R. Charles Loudermilk, Sr.
President Title:	Chairman/Chief Executive Officer
President Salutation:	Mr. Loudermilk
Industry Category (of 45):	37/Rental Services
IFA Member:	International Franchise Association
CFA Member:	

KEY FEATURES

- Number of Active North American Franchisors — ~ 2,300
  - % US — ~85%
  - % Canadian — ~15%
- Data Fields (See Above) — 24
- Industry Categories — 45
- % With Toll-Free Telephone Numbers — 67%
- % With Fax Numbers — 97%
- % With Name of Preferred Contact — 99%
- % With Name of President — 97%
- % With Number of Total Operating Units — 95%
- Guaranteed Accuracy — $.50 Rebate/Returned Bad Address
- Converted to Any Popular Database or Contact Management Program
- Initial Front-End Cost — $600
- Quarterly Up-Dates — $75
- Mailing Labels Only — One-Time Use — $400

For More Information, Please Contact
Source Book Publications
1814 Franklin Street, Suite 820, Oakland, California 94612
(800) 841-0873 ❖ (510) 839-5471 ❖ FAX (510) 839-2104

50 Proven Service-Based Winners

Bond's Top 50 Service-Based Franchises
by Steve Schiller and Robert Bond

Key Features:

In response to the constantly asked question, *"What are the best franchises?"*, Bond's newest book focuses on the top 50 franchises in the service industry. Over 500 service-based systems were evaluated for consideration. Companies were analyzed on the basis of historical performance, brand identification, market dynamics, franchisee satisfaction, the level of training and on-going support, financial stability, etc. Detailed 4–5 page profiles on each company, as well as key statistics and industry overviews. All companies are proven performers and most have a national presence. Excellent starting point for someone focusing on the service industry.

JUST PUBLISHED

Yes, I want to order ____ copy(ies) of *Bond's Top 50 Service-Based Franchises* at $19.95 each ($29.95 Canadian). Please add $4.00 per book for Shipping* & Handling ($5.75 Canada; International shipments at actual cost). California residents, please add appropriate sales tax.

Name _____ Title _____

Company _____ Telephone No. (____) _____

Address _____

City _____ State/Prov._____ Zip _____

❑ Check Enclosed or
Charge my: ❑ MasterCard ❑ Visa
Card #: _____ Expiration Date: _____
Signature: _____

Please return to: **Source Book Publications,** P.O. Box 12488, Oakland, CA 94604

* Note: All books shipped by USPS Priority Mail (2nd Day Air).
Satisfaction Guaranteed. If not fully satisfied, return for a prompt, 100% refund.

50 Proven Food-Service Winners

Bond's Top 50 Food-Service Franchises
by Steve Schiller and Robert Bond

Key Features:

In response to the constantly asked question, *"What are the best franchises?"*, Bond's newest book focuses on the top 50 franchises in the food-service industry. Over 500 food-service systems were evaluated for consideration. Companies were analyzed on the basis of historical performance, brand identification, market dynamics, franchisee satisfaction, the level of training and on-going support, financial stability, etc. Detailed 4–5 page profiles on each company, as well as key statistics and industry overviews. All companies are proven performers and most have a national presence. Excellent starting point for someone focusing on the food-service industry.

JUST PUBLISHED

Yes, I want to order ____ copy(ies) of *Bond's Top 50 Food-Service Franchises* at $19.95 each ($29.95 Canadian). Please add $4.00 per book for Shipping* & Handling ($5.75 Canada; International shipments at actual cost). California residents, please add appropriate sales tax.

Name _____ Title _____

Company _____ Telephone No. (____) _____

Address _____

City _____ State/Prov._____ Zip _____

❑   Check Enclosed or
Charge my: ❑   MasterCard   ❑   Visa

Card #: _____ Expiration Date: _____

Signature: _____

Please return to: **Source Book Publications,** P.O. Box 12488, Oakland, CA 94604

* Note: All books shipped by USPS Priority Mail (2nd Day Air).
Satisfaction Guaranteed. If not fully satisfied, return for a prompt, 100% refund.

The Definitive Franchising Directory

Bond's Franchise Guide
2002 (14th) Edition

Key Features:

- The Most Comprehensive and Up-To-Date Directory of Franchise Listings
- All New Data Every Edition
- Over 2,150 Total Listings
  1,050 Detailed Franchisor Profiles
  ~1,800 American Franchisors
  ~350 Canadian Franchisors
- 48 Distinct Business Categories
- Detailed Industry Statistics by Category
- 496 Pages (425 Pages of Franchise Listings)
- Direct Comparability Between Franchise Listings

PUBLISHED ANNUALLY

Yes, I want to order _____ copy(ies) of Bond's Franchise Guide at $29.95 each ($42.75 Canadian). Please add $4.00 per book for shipping * & handling ($5.75 Canada; International shipments at actual cost). California residents add appropriate sales tax.

Name _____ Title _____

Company _____ Telephone No. (_____) _____

Address _____

City _____ State/Prov. _____ Zip _____

❑   Check Enclosed or
Charge my: ❑   MasterCard ❑   Visa
Card #: _____ Expiration Date: _____
Signature: _____

Please send to: **Source Book Publications,** P.O. Box 12488, Oakland, CA 94604

* Note: All books shipped by USPS Priority Mail (2nd Day Air).
Satisfaction Guaranteed. If not fully satisfied, return for a prompt, 100% refund.